THE ORTHODOX WAY

by

Bishop Kallistos Ware

ST. VLADIMIR'S SEMINARY PRESS
CRESTWOOD, NY 10707–1699
1990

First published 1979 by A. R. Mowbray & Co. Ltd.,
Saint Thomas House, Becket Street,
Oxford, OX1 1SJ

Reprinted 1981
Reprinted 1986
Reprinted 1990

ISBN 0 913836 58 3

Printed in the United States of America
by Eerdmans Printing Co.

CONTENTS

Prologue Signposts on the Way   **7**

1 God as Mystery   12

2 God as Trinity   33

3 God as Creator   54

4 God as Man   88

5 God as Spirit   118

6 God as Prayer   140

Epilogue God as Eternity   178

Index of Authors and Sources   197

Index of Subjects   201

PROLOGUE

SIGNPOSTS ON THE WAY

I am the Way, the Truth and the Life.

John 14:6

The Church gives us not a system, but a key; not a plan of God's City, but the means of entering it. Perhaps someone will lose his way because he has no plan. But all that he will see, he will see without a mediator, he will see it directly, it will be real for him; while he who has studied only the plan risks remaining outside and not really finding anything.

Fr George Florovsky

One of the best known of the Desert Fathers of fourth-century Egypt, St Sarapion the Sindonite, travelled once on pilgrimage to Rome. Here he was told of a celebrated recluse, a woman who lived always in one small room, never going out. Sceptical about her way of life — for he was himself a great wanderer — Sarapion called on her and asked: 'Why are you sitting here?' To this she replied: 'I am not sitting. I am on a journey.'

I am not sitting. I am on a journey. Every Christian may apply these words to himself or herself. To be a Christian is to be a traveller. Our situation, say the Greek Fathers, is like that of the Israelite people in the desert of Sinai: we live in tents, not houses, for spiritually we are always on the move. We are on a journey through the inward space of the heart, a journey not measured by the hours of our watch or the days of the calendar, for it is a journey out of time into eternity.

One of the most ancient names for Christianity is simply 'the Way'. 'About that time', it is said in the Acts of the Apostles, 'there arose no little stir concerning the Way' (19:23); Felix, the Roman governor of Caesarea, had 'a rather accurate knowledge of the Way' (24:22). It is a name that emphasizes the practical character of the Christian faith. Christianity is more than a theory about the universe, more than teachings written down on paper; it is a path along which we journey — in the deepest and richest sense, the *way of life*.

There is only one means of discovering the true nature of Christianity. We must step out upon this path, commit ourselves to this way of life, and then we shall begin to *see for ourselves*. So long as we remain outside, we cannot properly understand. Certainly we need to be given directions before we start; we need to be told what signposts to look out for, and we need to have companions. Indeed, without guidance from others it is scarcely possible to begin the journey. But directions given by others can never convey to us what the way is actually like; they cannot be a substitute for direct, personal experience. Each is called to verify for himself what he has been taught, each is required to re-live the Tradition he has received. 'The Creed', said Metropolitan Philaret of Moscow, 'does not belong to you unless you have lived it.' No one can be an armchair traveller on this all-important journey. No one can be a Christian at second hand. God has children, but he has no grandchildren.

As a Christian of the Orthodox Church, I wish particularly to underline this need for *living experience*. To many in the twentieth-century West, the

Orthodox Church seems chiefly remarkable for its air of antiquity and conservatism; the message of the Orthodox to their Western brethren seems to be, 'We are your past'. For the Orthodox themselves, however, loyalty to Tradition means not primarily the acceptance of formulae or customs from past generations, but rather the ever-new, personal and direct experience of the Holy Spirit *in the present,* here and now.

Describing a visit to a country church in Greece, John Betjeman stresses the element of antiquity, but he also stresses something more:

> *. . . The domed interior swallows up the day.*
> *Here, where to light a candle is to pray,*
> *The candle flame shows up the almond eyes*
> *Of local saints who view with no surprise*
> *Their martyrdoms depicted upon walls*
> *On which the filtered daylight faintly falls.*
> *The flame shows up the cracked paint –*
> *   sea-green blue*
> *And red and gold, with grained wood showing*
> *   through –*
> *Of much kissed ikons, dating from, perhaps,*
> *The fourteenth century . . .*
> *Thus vigorously does the old tree grow,*
> *By persecution pruned, watered with blood,*
> *Its living roots deep in pre-Christian mud.*
> *It needs no bureaucratical protection.*
> *It is its own perpetual resurrection . . .*

Betjeman draws attention here to much that an Orthodox holds precious: the value of symbolic gestures such as the lighting of a candle; the role of ikons in conveying a sense of the local church as 'heaven on earth'; the prominence of martyrdom in the Orthodox experience – under the Turks since 1453, under the Communists since 1917. Orthodoxy in the modern world is indeed an 'old tree'. But besides age there is also vitality, a 'perpetual resurrection'; and it is this that matters, and not mere antiquity. Christ did not say, 'I am custom'; he said, 'I am the Life'.

It is the aim of the present book to uncover the deep sources of this 'perpetual resurrection'. The book indicates some of the decisive signposts and milestones upon the spiritual Way. No attempt is made here to provide a factual account of the past history and contemporary condition of the Orthodox world. Information on this can be found in my earlier work, *The Orthodox Church* (Penguin Books), originally published in 1963; and, so far as possible, I have avoided repeating what is said there.

My purpose in this present book is to offer a brief account of the fundamental teachings of the Orthodox Church, approaching the faith as a way of life and a way of prayer. Just as Tolstoy entitled one of his short stories, 'What men live by', so this book might have been called, 'What Orthodox Christians live by'. In an earlier and more formal epoch it might have taken the form of a 'catechism for adults', with questions and answers. But there is no attempt to be exhaustive. Very little is said here about the Church and its 'conciliar' character, about the communion of saints, the sacraments, the meaning of liturgical worship: perhaps I shall be able to make this the theme of another book. While referring occasionally to other Christian communions, I do not undertake any systematic comparisons. My concern is to describe in positive terms the faith by which as an Orthodox I live, rather than to suggest areas of concord or disagreement with Roman Catholicism or Protestantism.

Anxious that the voice of other and better witnesses should be heard besides my own, I have included many quotations, especially at the start and conclusion of each chapter. Brief notes on the authors and sources cited may be found at the end of the book. Most of the passages are from the Orthodox service books, used daily in our worship, or else from those whom we term the Fathers – writers mainly from the first eight centuries of Christian history, but in some cases later in date; for an author in our own day may also be a 'Father'. These quotations are the 'words' that have proved most helpful to me personally as signposts for my own explorations upon the Way. There are of course many other writers, not cited here by name, on whom I have also drawn.

O Saviour, who hast journeyed with Luke and Cleopas to Emmaus, journey with thy servants as they now set out upon their way, and defend them from all evil (Prayer before beginning a journey).

Feast of the Holy Apostle and Evangelist
John the Theologian, 26 September 1978

ARCHIMANDRITE KALLISTOS

CHAPTER 1

GOD AS MYSTERY

Unknown and yet well known.

2 Corinthians 6:9

God cannot be grasped by the mind. If he could be grasped, he would not be God.

Evagrius of Pontus

One day some of the brethren came to see Abba Antony, and among them was Abba Joseph. Wishing to test them, the old man mentioned a text from Scripture, and starting with the youngest he asked them what it meant. Each explained it as best he could. But to each one the old man said, 'You have not yet found the answer.' Last of all he said to Abba Joseph, 'And what do you think the text means?' He replied, 'I do not know.' Then Abba Antony said, 'Truly, Abba Joseph has found the way, for he said: I do not know.'

The Sayings of the Desert Fathers

As a friend talking with his friend, man speaks with God, and drawing near in confidence he stands before the face of the One who dwells in light unapproachable.

St Symeon the New Theologian

The Otherness yet Nearness of the Eternal

What or who is God?

The traveller upon the spiritual Way, the further

he advances, becomes increasingly conscious of two contrasting facts — of the *otherness* yet *nearness* of the Eternal. In the first place, he realizes more and more that God is *mystery*. God is 'the wholly Other', invisible, inconceivable, radically transcendent, beyond all words, beyond all understanding. 'Surely the babe just born', writes the Roman Catholic George Tyrrell, 'knows as much of the world and its ways as the wisest of us can know of the ways of God, whose sway stretches over heaven and earth, time and eternity.' A Christian in the Orthodox tradition will agree with this entirely. As the Greek Fathers insisted, 'A God who is comprehensible is not God.' A God, that is to say, whom we claim to understand exhaustively through the resources of our reasoning brain turns out to be no more than an idol, fashioned in our own image. Such a 'God' is most emphatically *not* the true and living God of the Bible and the Church. Man is made in God's image, but the reverse is not true.

Yet, in the second place, this God of mystery is at the same time uniquely close to us, filling all things, present everywhere around us and within us. And he is present, not merely as an atmosphere or nameless force, but in a personal way. The God who is infinitely beyond our understanding reveals himself to us as *person*: he calls us each by our name and we answer him. Between ourselves and the transcendent God there is a relationship of *love*, similar in kind to that between each of us and those other human beings dearest to us. We know other humans through our love for them, and through theirs for us. So it is also with God. In the words of Nicolas Cabasilas, God our King is

> *more affectionate than any friend,*
> *more just than any ruler,*
> *more loving than any father,*
> *more a part of us than our own limbs,*
> *more necessary to us than our own heart.*

These, then, are the two 'poles' in man's experience of the Divine. God is both further from us, and nearer to us, than anything else. And we find, paradoxically, that these two poles do not cancel one another out: on the contrary, the more we are attracted to the one 'pole', the more vividly we become aware of the other at the same time. Advancing on the Way, each finds that God grows ever more intimate and ever more distant, well known and yet unknown — well known to the smallest child, incomprehensible to the most brilliant theologian. God dwells in 'light unapproachable', yet man stands in his presence with loving confidence and addresses him as friend. God is both end-point and starting-point. He is the host who welcomes us at the conclusion of the journey, yet he is also the companion who walks by our side at every step upon the Way. As Nicolas Cabasilas puts it, 'He is both the inn at which we rest for a night and the final end of our journey.'

Mystery, yet person: let us consider these two aspects in turn.

God as Mystery

Unless we start out with a feeling of awe and astonishment — with what is often called a sense of the *numinous* — we shall make little progress on the Way. When Samuel Palmer first visited William Blake, the old man asked him how he approached the work of painting. 'With fear and trembling',

Palmer replied. 'Then you'll do', said Blake.

The Greek Fathers liken man's encounter with God to the experience of someone walking over the mountains in the mist: he takes a step forward and suddenly finds that he is on the edge of a precipice, with no solid ground beneath his foot but only a bottomless abyss. Or else they use the example of a man standing at night in a darkened room: he opens the shutter over a window, and as he looks out there is a sudden flash of lightning, causing him to stagger backwards, momentarily blinded. Such is the effect of coming face to face with the living mystery of God: we are assailed by dizziness; all the familiar footholds vanish, and there seems nothing for us to grasp; our inward eyes are blinded, our normal assumptions shattered.

The Fathers also take, as symbols of the spiritual Way, the two Old Testament figures of Abraham and Moses. Abraham, living still in his ancestral home at Ur of the Chaldees, is told by God: 'Go out from your country, and from your kindred, and from your father's house, to a land that I will show you' (Gen. 12:1). Accepting the divine call, he uproots himself from his familiar surroundings and ventures out into the unknown, without any clear conception of his final destination. He is simply commanded, 'Go out . . .', and in faith he obeys. Moses receives in succession three visions of God: first he sees God in a vision of light at the Burning Bush (Exod. 3:2); next God is revealed to him through mingled light and darkness, in the 'pillar of cloud and fire' which accompanies the people of Israel through the desert (Exod. 13:21); and then finally he meets God in a 'non-vision', when he speaks with him in the 'thick darkness' at the summit of Mount Sinai (Exod. 20:21).

Abraham journeys from his familiar home into

an unknown country; Moses progresses from light into darkness. And so it proves to be for each one who follows the spiritual Way. We go out from the known into the unknown, we advance from light into darkness. We do not simply proceed from the darkness of ignorance into the light of knowledge, but we go forward from the light of partial know-ledge into a greater knowledge which is so much more profound that it can only be described as the 'darkness of unknowing'. Like Socrates we begin to realize how little we understand. We see that it is not the task of Christianity to provide easy answers to every question, but to make us progressively aware of a mystery. God is not so much the object of our knowledge as the cause of our wonder. Quoting Psalm 8:1, 'O Lord, our Lord, how wonderful is thy name in all the earth', St Gregory of Nyssa states: 'God's name is not known; it is wondered at.'

Recognizing that God is incomparably greater than anything we can say or think about him, we find it necessary to refer to him not just through direct statements but through pictures and images. Our theology is to a large extent *symbolic*. Yet symbols alone are insufficient to convey the trans-cendence and the 'otherness' of God. To point at the *mysterium tremendum,* we need to use negative as well as affirmative statements, saying what God is *not* rather than what he is. Without this use of the way of negation, of what is termed the apophatic approach, our talk about God becomes gravely misleading. All that we affirm concerning God, however correct, falls far short of the living truth. If we say that he is good or just, we must at once add that his goodness or justice are not to be measured by our human standards. If we say that he exists, we must qualify this immediately by adding that he is not one existent object among many, that in his case the word 'exist' bears a unique significance. So the way of affirmation is balanced by the way of negation. As Cardinal Newman puts it, we are continually 'saying and unsaying to a positive effect'. Having made an assertion about God, we must pass beyond it: the statement is not untrue, yet neither it nor any other form of words can contain the fullness of the transcendent God.

So the spiritual Way proves to be a path of repentance in the most radical sense. *Metanoia,* the Greek word for repentance, means literally 'change of mind'. In approaching God, we are to change our mind, stripping ourselves of all our habitual ways of thinking. We are to be converted not only in our will but in our intellect. We need to reverse our interior perspective, to stand the pyramid on its head.

Yet the 'thick darkness' into which we enter with Moses turns out to be a luminous or dazzling darkness. The apophatic way of 'unknowing' brings us not to emptiness but to fullness. Our negations are in reality super-affirmations. Destructive in outward form, the apophatic approach is affirmative in its final effects: it helps us to reach out, beyond all statements positive or negative, beyond all language and all thought, towards an immediate experience of the living God.

This is implied, indeed, by the very word 'mystery'. In the proper religious sense of the term, 'mystery' signifies not only hiddenness but disclosure. The Greek noun *mysterion* is linked with the verb *myein,* meaning 'to close the eyes or mouth'. The candidate for initiation into certain of the pagan mystery religions was first blindfolded and led through a maze of passages; then suddenly his eyes were uncovered and he saw, displayed all round him, the secret emblems of the cult. So, in the Christian context, we do not mean by a 'mystery' merely that which is baffling and mysterious, an enigma or insoluble problem. A mystery is, on the contrary, something that is *revealed* for our understanding, but which we never understand *exhaustively* because it leads into the depth or the darkness of God. The eyes are closed — but they are also opened.

Thus, in speaking about God as mystery, we are brought to our second 'pole'. God is hidden from us, but he is also revealed to us: revealed as person and as love.

Faith in God as Person

In the Creed we do not say, 'I believe that there is a God'; we say, 'I believe in one God'. Between belief *that* and belief *in,* there is a crucial distinction. It is possible for me to believe *that* someone or something exists, and yet for this belief to have no practical effect upon my life. I can open the telephone directory for Wigan and scan the names recorded on its pages; and, as I read, I am prepared to believe that some (or even most) of these people actually exist. But I know none of them personally, I have never even visited Wigan, and so my belief that they exist makes no particular difference to me. When, on the other hand, I say to a much-loved friend, 'I *believe in* you', I am doing far more than expressing a belief that this person exists. 'I believe in you' means: I turn to you, I rely upon you, I put my full trust in you and I hope in you. And that is what we are saying to God in the Creed.

Faith in God, then, is not at all the same as the

kind of logical certainty that we attain in Euclidean geometry. God is not the conclusion to a process of reasoning, the solution to a mathematical problem. To believe in God is not to accept the possibility of his existence because it has been 'proved' to us by some theoretical argument, but it is to put our trust in One whom we know and love. Faith is not the supposition that something might be true, but the assurance that someone is there.

Because faith is not logical certainty but a personal relationship, and because this personal relationship is as yet very incomplete in each of us and needs continually to develop further, it is by no means impossible for faith to coexist with doubt. The two are not mutually exclusive. Perhaps there are some who by God's grace retain throughout their life the faith of a little child, enabling them to accept without question all that they have been taught. For most of those living in the West today, however, such an attitude is simply not possible. We have to make our own the cry, 'Lord, I believe: help my unbelief' (Mark 9:24). For very many of us this will remain our constant prayer right up to the very gates of death. Yet doubt does not in itself signify lack of faith. It may mean the opposite — that our faith is alive and growing. For faith implies not complacency but taking risks, not shutting ourselves off from the unknown but advancing boldly to meet it. Here an Orthodox Christian may readily make his own the words of Bishop J.A.T. Robinson: 'The act of faith is a constant dialogue with doubt.' As Thomas Merton rightly says, 'Faith is a principle of questioning and struggle before it becomes a principle of certitude and peace.'

Faith, then, signifies a personal relationship with God; a relationship as yet incomplete and faltering, yet none the less real. It is to know God not as a theory or an abstract principle, but as a person. To know a person is far more than to know facts about that person. To know a person is essentially to love him or her; there can be no true awareness of other persons without mutual love. We do not have any genuine knowledge of those whom we hate. Here, then, are the two least misleading ways of speaking about the God who surpasses our understanding: he is personal, and he is love. And these are basically two ways of saying the same thing. Our way of entry into the mystery of God is through personal love. As *The Cloud of Unknowing* says, 'He may well be loved, but not thought. By love can he be caught and held, but by thinking never.'

As a dim indication of this personal love prevailing between the believer and the Subject of his faith, let us take three examples or verbal ikons. The first is from the second-century account of St Polycarp's martyrdom. The Roman soldiers have just arrived to arrest the aged Bishop Polycarp, and to take him to what he knows must be his death:

When he heard that they had arrived, he came down and talked with them. All of them were amazed at his great age and his calmness, and they wondered why the authorities were so anxious to seize an old man like him. At once he gave orders that food and drink should be set before them, as much as they wanted, late though it was; and he asked them to allow him an hour in which to pray undisturbed. When they agreed, he stood up and prayed, and he was so filled with the grace of God that for two hours he could not keep silent. As they listened they were filled with amazement, and many of them regretted that they had come to arrest such a holy old man. He remembered by name all whom he had ever met, great and small, celebrated or unknown, and the whole Catholic Church throughout the world.

So all-consuming is his love for God, and for the whole of mankind in God, that at this moment of crisis St Polycarp thinks only of others and not of the danger to himself. When the Roman governor tells him to save his life by disowning Christ, he answers: 'Eighty-six years I have been his servant, and he has done me no wrong. How then can I blaspheme my King, who saved me?'

Secondly, here is St Symeon the New Theologian in the eleventh century, describing how Christ revealed himself in a vision of light:

You shone upon me with brilliant radiance and, so it seemed, you appeared to me in your wholeness as with my whole self I gazed openly upon you. And when I said, 'Master, who are you?' then you were pleased to speak for the first time with me the prodigal. With what gentleness did you talk to me, as I stood astonished and trembling, as I reflected a little within myself and said: 'What does this glory and this dazzling brightness mean? How is it that I am chosen to receive such great blessings?' 'I am God', you replied, 'who became man for your sake; and because you have sought me with your whole heart, see from this time onwards you shall be my brother, my fellow-heir, and my friend.'

Thirdly, here is a prayer by a seventeenth-century Russian bishop, St Dimitrii of Rostov:

Come, my Light, and illumine my darkness.
Come, my Life, and revive me from death.
Come, my Physician, and heal my wounds.
Come, Flame of divine love, and burn up the
    thorns of my sins, kindling my heart with the

flame of thy love.
Come, my King, sit upon the throne of my heart
    and reign there.
For thou alone art my King and my Lord.

Three 'Pointers'

God, then, is the One whom we love, our personal friend. We do not need to prove the existence of a personal friend. God, says Olivier Clément, 'is not exterior evidence, but the secret call within us'. If we believe in God, it is because we know him directly in our own experience, not because of logical proofs. A distinction, however, needs here to be made between 'experience' and 'experiences'. Direct experience can exist without necessarily being accompanied by specific experiences. There are indeed many who have come to believe in God because of some voice or vision, such as St Paul received on the road to Damascus (Acts 9:1-9). There are many others, however, who have never undergone particular experiences of this type, but who can yet affirm that, present throughout their life as a whole, there is a total experience of the living God, a conviction existing on a level more fundamental than all their doubts. Even though they cannot point to a precise place or moment in the way that St Augustine, Pascal or Wesley could, they can claim with confidence:*I know God personally.*

Such, then, is the basic 'evidence' of God's existence: an appeal to direct experience (but not necessarily to experiences). Yet, while there can be no logical demonstrations of the divine reality, there are certain 'pointers'. In the world around us, as also within ourselves, there are facts which cry out for an explanation, but which remain inexplicable unless we commit ourselves to belief in a personal God. Three such 'pointers' call for particular mention.

First, there is *the world around us*. What do we see? Much disorder and apparent waste, much tragic despair and seemingly useless suffering. And is that all? Surely not. If there is a 'problem of evil', there is also a 'problem of good'. Wherever we look, we see not only confusion but beauty. In snowflake, leaf or insect, we discover structured patterns of a delicacy and balance that nothing manufactured by human skill can equal. We are not to sentimentalize these things, but we cannot ignore them. How and why have these patterns emerged? If I take a pack of cards fresh from the factory, with the four suits neatly arranged in sequence, and I begin to shuffle it, then the more it is shuffled the more the initial pattern disappears and is replaced by a meaningless juxtaposition. But in the case of the universe the opposite has happened. Out of an initial chaos there have emerged patterns of an ever-increasing intricacy and meaning, and among all these patterns the most intricate and meaningful is man himself. Why should the process that happens to the pack of cards be precisely reversed on the level of the universe? What or who is responsible for this cosmic order and design? Such questions are not unreasonable. It is reason itself which impels me to search for an explanation whenever I discern order and meaning.

'The Corn was Orient and Immortal Wheat, which never should be reaped, nor was ever sown. I thought it had stood from Everlasting to Everlasting. The Dust and Stones of the Street were as Precious as Gold. . . The Green Trees when I saw them first through one of the Gates Transported

and Ravished me: their Sweetnes and unusual
Beauty made my Heart to leap, and almost mad
with Exstasie, they were such strange and Wonderful Things. . .' Thomas Traherne's childhood
apprehensions of the beauty of the world can be
paralleled by numerous texts from Orthodox
sources. Here, for example, are the words of Prince
Vladimir Monomakh of Kiev:

*See how the sky, the sun and moon and stars, the
darkness and light, and the earth that is laid upon the
waters, are ordered, O Lord, by thy providence! See
how the different animals, and the birds and fishes,
are adorned through thy loving care, O Lord! This
wonder, also, we admire: how thou hast created man
out of the dust and how varied is the appearance of
human faces: though we should gather together all
men throughout the whole world, yet there is none
with the same appearance, but each by God's wisdom has his own appearance. Let us also marvel
how the birds of the sky go out from their paradise:
they do not stay in one country but go, strong and
weak alike, over all countries at God's command, to
all forests and fields.*

This presence of meaning within the world as well
as confusion, of coherence and beauty as well as
futility, provides us with a first 'pointer' towards
God. We find a second 'pointer' *within ourselves*.
Why, distinct from my desire for pleasure and dis-
like of pain, do I have within myself a feeling of
duty and moral obligation, a sense of right and
wrong, a conscience? And this conscience does not
simply tell me to obey standards taught to me by

others; it is personal. Why, furthermore, placed as I am within time and space, do I find within myself what Nicolas Cabasilas calls an 'infinite thirst' or thirst for what is infinite? Who am I? What am I?

The answer to these questions is far from obvious. The boundaries of the human person are extremely wide; each of us knows very little about his true and deep self. Through our faculties of perception, outward and inward, through our memory and through the power of the unconscious, we range widely over space, we stretch backward and forward in time, and we reach out beyond space and time into eternity. 'Within the heart are unfathomable depths', affirm *The Homilies of St Macarius*. 'It is but a small vessel: and yet dragons and lions are there, and there poisonous creatures and all the treasures of wickedness; rough, uneven paths are there, and gaping chasms. There likewise is God, there are the angels, there life and the Kingdom, there light and the Apostles, the heavenly cities and the treasures of grace: all things are there.'

In this manner we have, each within our own heart, a second 'pointer'. What is the meaning of my conscience? What is the explanation for my sense of the infinite? Within myself there is something which continually makes me look beyond myself. Within myself I bear a source of wonder, a source of constant self-transcendence.

A third 'pointer' is to be found in my *relationships with other human persons*. For each of us — perhaps once or twice only in the whole course of our life — there have been sudden moments of discovery when we have seen disclosed the deepest being and truth of another, and we have experienced his or her inner life as if it were our own. And this encounter with the true personhood of another is, once more, a contact with the transcendent and timeless, with something stronger than death. To say to another, with all our heart, 'I love you', is to say, 'You will never die'. At such moments of personal sharing we know, not through arguments but by immediate conviction, that there is life beyond death. So it is that in our relations with others, as in our experience of ourselves, we have moments of transcendence, pointing to something that lies beyond. How are we to be loyal to these moments, and to make sense of them?

These three 'pointers' — in the world around us, in the world within us, and in our inter-personal relationships — can serve together as a way of approach, bringing us to the threshold of faith in God. None of these 'pointers' constitutes a logical proof. But what is the alternative? Are we to say that the apparent order in the universe is mere coincidence; that conscience is simply the result of social conditioning; and that, when life on this planet finally becomes extinct, all that humankind has experienced and all our potentialities will be as though they had never existed? Such an answer seems to me not only unsatisfying and inhuman, but also extremely unreasonable.

It is fundamental to my character as a human being that I search everywhere for meaningful explanations. I do this with the smaller things in my life: shall I not do this also with the greater? Belief in God helps me to understand why the world should be as it is, with its beauty as well as its ugliness; why I should be as I am, with my nobility as well as my meanness; and why I should love others, affirming their eternal value. Apart from belief in God I can see no other explanation for all this. *Faith in God enables me to make sense of things, to see them as a coherent whole, in a way that nothing else can do.* Faith enables me to make one out of the many.

Essence and Energies

To indicate the two 'poles' of God's relationship to us — unknown yet well known, hidden yet revealed — the Orthodox tradition draws a distinction between the essence, nature or inner being of God, on the one hand, and his energies, operations or acts of power, on the other.

'He is outside all things according to his essence', writes St Athanasius, 'but he is in all things through his acts of power.' 'We know the essence through the energy', St Basil affirms. 'No one has ever seen the essence of God, but we believe in the essence because we experience the energy.' By the essence of God is meant his otherness, by the energies his nearness. Because God is a mystery beyond our understanding, we shall never know his essence or inner being, either in this life or in the Age to come. If we knew the divine essence, it would follow that we knew God in the same way as he knows himself; and this we cannot ever do, since he is Creator and we are created. But, while God's inner essence is for ever beyond our comprehension, his energies, grace, life and power fill the whole universe, and are directly accessible to us.

The essence, then, signifies the radical transcendence of God; the energies, his immanence and omnipresence. When Orthodox speak of the divine energies, they do not mean by this an emanation from God, an 'intermediary' between God and man, or a 'thing' or 'gift' that God bestows. On the contrary, the energies are God himself in his activity and self-manifestation. When a man knows or participates in the divine energies, he truly knows or participates in God himself, so far as this is possible for a created being. But God is God, and we are men; and so, while he possesses us, we cannot in the same way possess him.

Just as it would be wrong to think of the energies as a 'thing' bestowed on us by God, so it would be equally misleading to regard the energies as a 'part'· of God. The Godhead is simple and indivisible, and has no parts. The essence signifies the whole God as he is in himself; the energies signify the whole God as he is in action. God in his entirety is completely present in each of his divine energies. Thus the essence-energies distinction is a way of stating simultaneously that the *whole* God is inaccessible, and that the *whole* God in his outgoing love has rendered himself accessible to man.

By virtue of this distinction between the divine essence and the divine energies, we are able to affirm the possibility of a direct or mystical union between man and God — what the Greek Fathers term the *theosis* of man, his 'deification' — but at the same time we exclude any pantheistic identification between the two: for man participates in the energies of God, not in the essence. There is union, but not fusion or confusion. Although 'oned' with the divine, man still remains man; he is not swallowed up or annihilated, but between him and God there continues always to exist an 'I – Thou' relationship of person to person.

Such, then, is our God: unknowable in his essence, yet known in his energies; beyond and above all that we can think or express, yet closer to us than our own heart. Through the apophatic way we smash in pieces all the idols or mental images that we form of him, for we know that all are unworthy of his surpassing greatness. Yet at the same time, through our prayer and through our active service in the world, we discover at every moment his divine energies, his immediate presence in each person and each thing. Daily, hourly we touch him. We are, as Francis Thompson said, 'in no strange land'. All around us is the 'many-splendoured thing'; Jacob's ladder is 'pitched betwixt heaven and Charing Cross':

O world invisible, we view thee,
O world intangible, we touch thee,
O world unknowable, we know thee,
Inapprehensible, we clutch thee.

In the words of John Scotus Eriugena, 'Every visible or invisible creature is a theophany or appearance of God.' The Christian is the one who, wherever he looks, sees God everywhere and rejoices in him. Not without reason did the early Christians attribute to Christ this saying: 'Lift the stone and you will find me; cut the wood in two and there am I.'

Imagine a sheer, steep crag, with a projecting edge at the top. Now imagine what a person would probably feel if he put his foot on the edge of this precipice and, looking down into the chasm below, saw no solid footing nor anything to hold on to. This is what I think the soul experiences when it goes beyond its footing in material things, in its quest for that which has no dimension and which exists from all eternity. For here there is nothing it can take hold of, neither place nor time, neither measure nor anything else;

our minds cannot approach it. And thus the soul, slipping at every point from what cannot be grasped, becomes dizzy and perplexed and returns once again to what is connatural to it, content now to know merely this about the Transcendent, that it is completely different from the nature of the things that the soul knows.

St Gregory of Nyssa

Think of a man standing at night inside his house, with all the doors closed; and then suppose that he opens a window just at the moment when there is a sudden flash of lightning. Unable to bear its brightness, at once he protects himself by closing his eyes and drawing back from the window. So it is with the soul that is enclosed in the realm of the senses: if ever she peeps out through the window of the intellect, she is overwhelmed by the brightness, like lightning, of the pledge of the Holy Spirit that is within her. Unable to bear the splendour of unveiled light, at once she is bewildered in her intellect and she draws back entirely upon herself, taking refuge, as in a house, among sensory and human things.

St Symeon the New Theologian

Anyone who tries to describe the ineffable Light in language is truly a liar — not because he hates the truth, but because of the inadequacy of his description.

St Gregory of Nyssa

Leave the senses and the workings of the intellect, and all that the senses and the intellect can perceive, and all that is not and that is; and through unknowing reach out, so far as this is possible, towards oneness with him who is beyond all being and know-

ledge. In this way, through an uncompromising, absolute and pure detachment from yourself and from all things, transcending all things and released from all, you will be led upwards towards that radiance of the divine darkness which is beyond all being.

Entering the darkness that surpasses ·understanding, we shall find ourselves brought, not just to brevity of speech, but to perfect silence and unknowing.

Emptied of all knowledge, man is joined in the highest part of himself, not with any created thing, nor with himself, nor with another, but with the One who is altogether unknowable; and, in knowing nothing, he knows in a manner that surpasses understanding.

St Dionysius the Areopagite

The form of God is ineffable and indescribable, and cannot be seen with eyes of flesh. He is in glory uncontainable, in greatness incomprehensible, in loftiness inconceivable, in strength incomparable, in wisdom inaccessible, in love inimitable, in beneficence inexpressible.

Just as the soul in a man is not seen, since it is invisible to men, but we know of its existence through the movements of the body, so God cannot be seen by human eyes, but he is seen and known through his providence and his works.

Theophilus of Antioch

We do not know God in his essence. We know him rather from the grandeur of his creation and from his providential care for all creatures. For by this means, as if using a mirror, we attain insight into his infinite goodness, wisdom and power.

St Maximus the Confessor

The most important thing that happens between God and the human soul is to love and to be loved.
Kallistos Kataphygiotis

Love for God is ecstatic, making us go out from ourselves: it does not allow the lover to belong any more to himself, but he belongs only to the Beloved.
St Dionysius the Areopagite

I know that the Immovable comes down;
I know that the Invisible appears to me;
I know that he who is far outside the whole creation
Takes me within himself and hides me in his arms,
And then I find myself outside the whole world.
I, a frail, small mortal in the world,
Behold the Creator of the world, all of him, within myself;
And I know that I shall not die, for I am within the Life,
I have the whole of Life springing up as a fountain within me.
He is in my heart, he is in heaven:
Both there and here he shows himself to me with equal glory.
St Symeon the New Theologian

CHAPTER 2

GOD AS TRINITY

O Father, my hope:
O Son, my refuge:
O Holy Spirit, my protection:
Holy Trinity, glory to thee.

Prayer of St Ioannikios

O Trinity, uncreated and without beginning,
O undivided Unity, three and one,
Father, Son and Spirit, a single God:
Accept this our hymn from tongues of clay
As if from mouths of flame.

From the Lenten Triodion

God as Mutual Love

'I believe in one God': so we affirm at the beginning of the Creed. But then at once we go on to say much more than this. I believe, we continue, in one God who is at the same time three, Father, Son and Holy Spirit. There is in God genuine diversity as well as true unity. The Christian God is not just a unit but a union, not just unity but community. There is in God something analogous to 'society'. He is not a single person, loving himself alone, not a self-contained monad or 'The One'. He is triunity: three equal persons, each one dwelling in the other two by virtue of an unceasing movement of mutual love. *Amo ergo sum*, 'I love, therefore I am': the title of Kathleen Raine's poem can serve as a motto for God the Holy Trinity. What Shakespeare says concerning the human love of two may be applied also to the divine love of the eternal Three:

> *So they loved, as love in twain,*
> *Had the essence but in one;*
> *Two distincts, division none:*
> *Number there in love was slain.*

The final end of the spiritual Way is that we humans should also become part of this Trinitarian coinherence or *perichoresis,* being wholly taken up into the circle of love that exists within God. So Christ prayed to his Father on the night before his Crucifixion: 'May they all be one: as thou, Father, art in me, and I in thee, so may they also be one in us' (John 17:21).

Why believe that God is three? Is it not easier to believe simply in the divine unity, as the Jews and the Mohammedans do? Certainly it is easier. The doctrine of the Trinity stands before us as a challenge, as a 'crux' in the literal sense: it is, in Vladimir Lossky's words, 'a cross for human ways of thought', and it requires from us a radical act of *metanoia* — not merely a gesture of formal assent, but a true change of mind and heart.

Why, then, believe in God as Trinity? In the last chapter we found that the two most helpful ways of entry into the divine mystery are to affirm that God is *personal* and that God is *love.* Now both these notions imply sharing and reciprocity. First, a 'person' is not at all the same as an 'individual'. Isolated, self-dependent, none of us is an authentic person but merely an individual, a bare unit as recorded in the census. Egocentricity is the death of true personhood. Each becomes a real person only through entering into relation with other persons, through living for them and in them. There can be no man, so it has been rightly said, until there are at least two men in communication. The same is true, secondly, of love. Love cannot exist in isolation, but presupposes the other. Self-love is the negation of love. As Charles Williams shows to such devastating effect in his novel *Descent into Hell*, self-love is hell; for, carried to its ultimate conclusion, self-love signifies the end of all joy and all meaning. Hell is not other people; hell is myself, cut off from others in self-centredness.

God is far better than the best that we know in ourselves. If the most precious element in our human life is the relationship of 'I and Thou', then we cannot but ascribe this same relationship, in some sense, to the eternal being of God himself. And that is precisely what the doctrine of the Holy Trinity means. At the very heart of the divine life, from all eternity God knows himself as 'I and Thou' in a threefold way, and he rejoices continually in this knowledge. All, then, that is implied in our limited understanding of the human person and of human love, this we affirm also of God the Trinity, while adding that in him these things mean infinitely more than we can ever imagine.

Personhood and love signify life, movement, discovery. So the doctrine of the Trinity means that we should think of God in terms that are dynamic rather than static. God is not just stillness, repose, unchanging perfection. For our images of the Trinitarian God we should look rather to the wind, to the running water, to the unresting flames of fire. A favourite analogy for the Trinity has always been that of three torches burning with a single flame. We are told in *The Sayings of the Desert Fathers* how a brother once came to talk with Abba Joseph of Panepho. 'Abba', said the visitor, 'according to my strength I observe a modest rule of prayer and fasting, of reading and silence, and so far as I can I keep myself pure in my thoughts. What more can I do?' In answer, Abba Joseph rose to his feet and held up his hands towards the sky; and his fingers became as ten blazing torches. And the old man said to the brother: 'If you wish, you can become completely as a flame.' If this image of the living flame helps us to understand man's nature at its highest, can it not also be applied to God? The three persons of the Trinity are 'completely as a flame'.

But in the end the least misleading ikon is to be found, not in the physical world outside us, but in the human heart. The best analogy is that with which we began: our experience of caring intensely for another person, and of knowing that our love is returned.

Three Persons in One Essence

'I and the Father are one', said Christ (John 10:30). What did he mean?

For an answer we look primarily to the first two of the seven Ecumenical or Universal Councils: to the Council of Nicaea (325), to the first Council of Constantinople (381), and to the Creed which they formulated. The central and decisive affirmation in the Creed is that Jesus Christ is 'true God from true God', 'one in essence' or 'consubstantial' (*homoousios*) with God the Father. In other words, Jesus Christ is equal to the Father: he is God in the same sense that the Father is God, and yet they are not two Gods but one. Developing this teaching, the Greek Fathers of the later fourth century said the same about the Holy Spirit: he is likewise truly God, 'one in essence' with the Father and the Son. But although Father, Son and Spirit are one single

God, yet each of them is from all eternity a person, a distinct centre of conscious selfhood. God the Trinity is thus to be described as 'three persons in one essence'. There is eternally in God true unity, combined with genuinely personal differentiation: the term 'essence', 'substance' or 'being' (*ousia*) indicates the unity, and the term 'person' (*hypostasis, prosopon*) indicates the differentiation. Let us try to understand what is signified by this somewhat baffling language, for the dogma of the Holy Trinity is vital to our own salvation.

Father, Son and Spirit are one in essence, not merely in the sense that all three are examples of the same group or general class, but in the sense that they form a single, unique, specific reality. There is in this respect an important difference between the sense in which the three divine persons are one, and the sense in which three human persons may be termed one. Three human persons, Peter, James and John, belong to the same general class 'man'. Yet, however closely they co-operate together, each retains his own will and his own energy, acting by virtue of his own separate power of initiative. In short, they are three men and not one man. But in the case of the three persons of the Trinity, this is not the case. There is distinction, but never separation. Father, Son and Spirit — so the saints affirm, following the testimony of Scripture — have only one will and not three, only one energy and not three. None of the three ever acts separately, apart from the other two. They are not three Gods, but one God.

Yet, although the three persons never act apart from each other, there is in God genuine diversity as well as specific unity. In our experience of God at work within our own life, while we find that the three are always acting together, yet we know that each is acting within us in a different manner. We experience God as three-in-one, and we believe that this threefold differentiation in God's outward action reflects a threefold differentiation in his inner life. The distinction between the three persons is to be regarded as an eternal distinction existing within the nature of God himself; it does not apply merely to his exterior activity in the world. Father, Son and Spirit are not just 'modes' or 'moods' of the Divinity, not just masks which God assumes for a time in his dealings with creation and then lays aside. They are on the contrary three coequal and coeternal persons. A human father is older than his child, but when speaking of God as 'Father' and 'Son' we are not to interpret the terms in this literal sense. We affirm of the Son, 'There never was a time when he was not'. And the same is said of the Spirit.

Each of the three is fully and completely God. None is more or less God than the others. Each possesses, not one third of the Godhead, but the entire Godhead in its totality; yet each lives and is this one Godhead in his own distinctive and personal way. Stressing this Trinitarian unity-in-diversity, St Gregory of Nyssa writes:

All that the Father is, we see revealed in the Son; all that is the Son's is the Father's also; for the whole Son dwells in the Father, and he has the whole Father dwelling in himself. . . The Son who exists always in the Father can never be separated from him, nor can the Spirit ever be divided from the Son who through the Spirit works all things. He who receives the Father also receives at the same time the Son and the Spirit. It is impossible to envisage any kind of severance or disjunction between them: one cannot think of the Son apart from the Father, nor divide the Spirit from the Son. There is between the three a sharing and a differentiation that are beyond words and understanding. The distinction between the persons does not impair the oneness of nature, nor does the shared unity of essence lead to a confusion between the distinctive characteristics of the persons. Do not be surprised that we should speak of the Godhead as being at the same time both unified and differentiated. Using riddles, as it were, we envisage a strange and paradoxical diversity-in-unity and unity-in-diversity.

'Using riddles..': St Gregory is at pains to emphasize that the doctrine of the Trinity is 'paradoxical' and lies 'beyond words and understanding'. It is something revealed to us by God, not demonstrated to us by our own reason. We can hint at it in human language, but we cannot fully explain it. Our reasoning powers are a gift from God, and we must use them to the full; but we should recognize their limitations. The Trinity is not a philosophical theory but the living God whom we worship; and so there comes a point in our approach to the Trinity when argumentation and analysis must give place to wordless prayer. 'Let all mortal flesh keep silent, and stand with fear and trembling' (The Liturgy of St James).

Personal Characteristics

The first person of the Trinity, God the Father, is the 'fountain' of the Godhead, the source, cause or principle of origin for the other two persons. He is the bond of unity between the three: there is one God because there is one Father. 'The union is the

Father, from whom and to whom the order of the persons runs its course' (St Gregory the Theologian). The other two persons are each defined in terms of their relationship to the Father: the Son is 'begotten' by the Father, the Spirit 'proceeds' from the Father. In the Latin West, it is usually held that the Spirit proceeds 'from the Father and from the Son'; and the word *filioque* ('and from the Son') has been added to the Latin text of the Creed. Orthodoxy not only regards the *filioque* as an unauthorized addition — for it was inserted into the Creed without the consent of the Christian East — but it also considers that the doctrine of the 'double procession', as commonly expounded, is theologically inexact and spiritually harmful. According to the Greek Fathers of the fourth century, whom the Orthodox Church follows to this day, the Father is the sole source and ground of unity in the Godhead. To make the Son a source as well as the Father, or in combination with him, is to risk confusing the distinctive characteristics of the persons.

The second person of the Trinity is the Son of God, his 'Word' or Logos. To speak in this way of God as Son and Father is at once to imply a movement of mutual love, such as we indicated earlier. It is to imply that from all eternity God himself, as Son, in filial obedience and love renders back to God the Father the being which the Father by paternal self-giving eternally generates in him. It is in and through the Son that the Father is revealed to us: 'I am the Way, the Truth and the Life: no one comes to the Father, except through me' (John 14:6). He it is who was born on earth as man, from the Virgin Mary in the city of Bethlehem. But as Word or Logos of God he is also at work before the Incarnation. He is the principle of order and purpose that permeates all things, drawing them to unity in God, and so making the universe into a 'cosmos', a harmonious and integrated whole. The Creator-Logos has imparted to each created thing its own indwelling *logos* or inner principle, which makes that thing to be distinctively itself, and which at the same time draws and directs that thing towards God. Our human task as craftsmen or manufacturers is to discern this *logos* dwelling in each thing and to render it manifest; we seek not to dominate but to co-operate.

The third person is the Holy Spirit, the 'wind' or 'breath' of God. While appreciating the inadequacy of neat classifications, we may say that the Spirit is God *within us,* the Son is God *with us,* and the Father God *above or beyond us.* Just as the Son shows us the Father, so it is the Spirit who shows us the Son, making him present to us. Yet the relation is mutual. The Spirit makes the Son present to us, but it is the Son who sends us the Spirit. (We note that there is a distinction between the 'eternal procession' of the Spirit and his 'temporal mission'. The Spirit is sent into the world, within time, by the Son; but, as regards his origin within the eternal life of the Trinity, the Spirit proceeds from the Father alone.)

Characterizing each of the three persons, Synesius of Cyrene writes:

Hail, Father, source of the Son,
Son, the Father's image;
Father, the ground where the Son stands,
Son, the Father's seal;
Father, the power of the Son,
Son, the Father's beauty;
All-pure Spirit, bond between

the Father and the Son.
Send, O Christ, the Spirit, send
the Father to my soul;
Steep my dry heart in this dew,
the best of all thy gifts.

Why speak of God as Father and Son, and not as Mother and Daughter? In itself the Godhead possesses neither maleness nor femininity. Although our human sexual characteristics as male and female reflect, at their highest and truest, an aspect of the divine life, yet there is in God no such thing as sexuality. When, therefore, we speak of God as Father, we are speaking not literally but in symbols. Yet why should the symbols be masculine rather than feminine? Why call God 'he' and not 'she'? In fact, Christians have sometimes applied 'mother language' to God. Aphrahat, one of the early Syriac Fathers, speaks of the believer's love for 'God his Father and the Holy Spirit his Mother', while in the medieval West we find the Lady Julian of Norwich affirming: 'God rejoices that he is our Father, and God rejoices that he is our Mother.' But these are exceptions. Almost always the symbolism used of God by the Bible and in the Church's worship has been male symbolism.

We cannot prove by arguments why this should be so, yet it remains a fact of our Christian experience that God has set his seal upon certain symbols and not upon others. The symbols are not chosen by us but revealed and *given*. A symbol can be verified, lived, prayed — but not 'proved' logically. These 'given' symbols, however, while not capable of proof, are yet far from being arbitrary. Like the symbols in myth, literature and art, our religious symbols reach deep into the hidden roots of our being, and cannot be altered without momentous consequences. If, for example, we were to start saying 'Our Mother who art in heaven', instead of 'Our Father', we should not merely be adjusting an incidental piece of imagery, but replacing Christianity with a new kind of religion. A Mother Goddess is not the Lord of the Christian Church.

Why should God be a communion of three divine persons, neither less nor more? Here again there can be no logical proof. The threeness of God is something given or revealed to us in Scripture, in the Apostolic Tradition, and in the experience of the saints throughout the centuries. All that we can do is to *verify* this given fact through our own life of prayer.

What precisely is the difference between the 'generation' of the Son and the 'procession' of the Spirit? 'The manner of the generation and the manner of the procession are incomprehensible', says St John of Damascus. 'We have been told that there is a difference between generation and procession, but what is the nature of this difference, we do not understand at all.' If St John of Damascus confessed himself baffled, then so may we. The terms 'generation' and 'procession' are conventional signs for a reality far beyond the comprehension of our reasoning brain. 'Our reasoning brain is weak, and our tongue is weaker still', remarks St Basil the Great. 'It is easier to measure the entire sea with a tiny cup than to grasp God's ineffable greatness with the human mind.' But, while they cannot be fully explained, these signs can (as we have said) be verified. Through our encounter with God in prayer, we *know* that the Spirit is not the same as the Son, even though we cannot define in words precisely what the difference is.

The Two Hands of God

Let us try to illustrate the doctrine of the Trinity by looking at the Triadic patterns in salvation history and in our own life of prayer.

The three persons, as we saw, work always together, and possess but a single will and energy. St Irenaeus speaks of the Son and the Spirit as the 'two hands' of God the Father; and in every creative and sanctifying act the Father is using both these 'hands' at once. Scripture and worship provide repeated examples of this:

1. *Creation.* 'By the Word of the Lord were the heavens made, and all the host of them by the Breath of his mouth' (Ps. 33:6). God the Father creates through his 'Word' or Logos (the second person) and through his 'Breath' or Spirit (the third person). The 'two hands' of the Father work together in the shaping of the universe. Of the Logos it is said, 'all things were made through him' (John 1:3: compare the Creed, ' . . . through whom all things were made'); of the Spirit it is said that at the creation he 'brooded' or 'moved upon the face of the deep' (Gen. 1:2). All created things are marked with the seal of the Trinity.

2. *Incarnation.* At the Annunciation the Father sends the Holy Spirit upon the Blessed Virgin Mary, and she conceives the eternal Son of God (Luke 1:35). So God's taking of our humanity is a Trinitarian work. The Spirit is sent down from the Father, to effect the Son's presence within the womb of the Virgin. The Incarnation, it should be added, is not only the work of the Trinity but also the work of Mary's free will. God waited for her

voluntary consent, expressed in the words, 'Behold, the handmaid of the Lord: be it unto me according to thy word' (Luke 1:38); and had this consent been withheld, Mary would not have become God's Mother. Divine grace does not destroy human freedom but reaffirms it.

3. *The Baptism of Christ.* In the Orthodox tradition this is seen as a revelation of the Trinity. The Father's voice from heaven bears witness to the Son, saying, 'This is my beloved Son, in whom I am well pleased'; and at the same moment the Holy Spirit, in the form of a dove, descends from the Father and rests upon the Son (Matt. 3:16-17). So the Orthodox Church sings at Epiphany (6 January), the feast of Christ's Baptism:

When thou, O Lord, wast baptized in the Jordan,
The worship of the Trinity was made manifest.
For the voice of the Father bore witness unto thee,
Calling thee the beloved Son,
And the Spirit in the form of a dove
Confirmed his word as sure and steadfast.

4. *The Transfiguration of Christ.* This also is a Trinitarian happening. The same relationship prevails between the three persons as at the Baptism. The Father testifies from heaven, 'This is my beloved Son, in whom I am well pleased; hear him' (Matt. 17:5), while as before the Spirit descends upon the Son, this time in the form of a cloud of light (Luke 9:34). As we affirm in one of the hymns for this feast (6 August):

Today on Tabor in the manifestation of thy light,
*   O Lord,*
Thou light unaltered from the light of the un-
*   begotten Father,*
We have seen the Father as light,

And the Spirit as light,
Guiding with light the whole creation.

5. *The Eucharistic Epiclesis.* The same Triadic pattern as is evident at the Annunciation, the Baptism and the Transfiguration, is apparent likewise at the culminating moment of the Eucharist, the *epiclesis* or invocation of the Holy Spirit. In words addressed to the Father, the celebrant priest says in the Liturgy of St John Chrysostom:

We offer to thee this spiritual worship without shedding of blood,
And we pray and beseech and implore thee:
Send down thy Holy Spirit upon us and upon these gifts here set forth:
And make this bread the precious Body of thy Christ,
And what is in this cup the precious Blood of thy Christ,
Transforming them by thy Holy Spirit.

As at the Annunciation, so in the extension of Christ's Incarnation at the Eucharist, the Father sends down the Holy Spirit, to effect the Son's presence in the consecrated gifts. Here, as always, the three persons of the Trinity are working together.

Praying the Trinity

As there is a Triadic structure in the eucharistic *epiclesis,* so there is likewise in almost all the prayers of the Church. The opening invocations, used by Orthodox at their daily prayers each morning and evening, have an unmistakably Trinitarian spirit. So familiar are these prayers, so frequently repeated, that it is easy to overlook their true character as glorification of the Holy Trinity. We begin by confessing God three-in-one, as we make the sign of the Cross with the words:

In the name of the Father, and of the Son, and of the Holy Spirit.

So, at the very beginning of each new day, we place it under the protection of the Trinity. Next we say, 'Glory to thee, our God, glory to thee' — the new day begins with celebration, joy, thanksgiving. This is followed by a prayer to the Holy Spirit, 'O heavenly King. . .' Then we repeat three times:

Holy God,
Holy and Strong,
Holy and Immortal,
*   have mercy upon us.*

The threefold 'holy' recalls the hymn 'Holy, holy, holy', sung by the seraphim in Isaiah's vision (Isa. 6:3), and by the four apocalyptic beasts in the Revelation of St John the Divine (Rev. 4:8). In this thrice-repeated 'holy' there is an invocation of the eternal Three. This is followed, in our daily prayers, by the most frequent of all liturgical phrases, 'Glory be to the Father, and to the Son, and to the Holy Spirit. . .' Here, above all, we must not allow familiarity to breed contempt. Each time this phrase is used, it is vital to recall its true meaning as a giving of glory to the Triunity. The *Gloria* is succeeded by another prayer to the three persons:

Most Holy Trinity, have mercy upon us.
O Lord, cleanse us from our sins.
O Master, pardon our iniquities.
O Holy One, visit and heal our infirmities
*   for thy name's sake.*

So our daily prayers continue. At each step, implicitly or explicitly, there is a Triadic structure, a proclamation of God as one-in-three. We think the Trinity, speak the Trinity, breathe the Trinity.

There is a Trinitarian dimension also to the most dearly-loved of single-phrase Orthodox prayers, the Jesus Prayer, an 'arrow prayer' used both at work and during times of quiet. In its most common form this runs:

> *Lord Jesus Christ, Son of God, have mercy on me a sinner.*

This is, in outward form, a prayer to the second person of the Trinity, the Lord Jesus Christ. But the other two persons are also present, although they are not named. For, by speaking of Jesus as 'Son of God', we point towards his Father; and the Spirit is also embraced in our prayer, since 'no one can say "Lord Jesus", except in the Holy Spirit' (1 Cor. 12:3). The Jesus Prayer is not only Christ-centred but Trinitarian.

Living the Trinity

'Prayer is action' (Tito Colliander). 'What is pure prayer? Prayer which is brief in words but abundant in actions. For if your actions do not exceed your petitions, then your prayers are mere words, and the seed of the hands is not in them' (*The Sayings of the Desert Fathers*).

If prayer is to be transmuted into action, then this Trinitarian faith which informs all our praying must also be manifest in our daily life. Immediately before reciting the Creed in the Eucharistic Liturgy, we say these words: 'Let us love one another, so that we may with one mind confess Father, Son and Holy Spirit, the Trinity one in essence and undivided.' Note the words 'so that'. A genuine confession of faith in the Triune God can be made only by those who, after the likeness of the Trinity, show love mutually towards each other. There is an integral connection between our love for one another and our faith in the Trinity: the first is a precondition for the second, and in its turn the second gives full strength and meaning to the first.

So far from being pushed into the corner and treated as a piece of abstruse theologizing of interest only to specialists, the doctrine of the Trinity ought to have upon our daily life an effect that is nothing less than revolutionary. Made after the image of God the Trinity, human beings are called to reproduce on earth the mystery of mutual love that the Trinity lives in heaven. In medieval Russia St Sergius of Radonezh dedicated his newly-founded monastery to the Holy Trinity, precisely because he intended that his monks should show towards one another day by day the same love as passes between the three divine persons. And such is the vocation not only of monks but of everyone. Each social unit — the family, the school, the work-shop, the parish, the Church universal — is to be made an ikon of the Triunity. Because we know that God is three in one, each of us is committed to living sacrificially in and for the other; each is committed irrevocably to a life of practical service, of active compassion. Our faith in the Trinity puts us under an obligation to struggle at every level, from the strictly personal to the highly organized, against all forms of oppression, injustice and exploitation. In our combat for social righteousness and 'human rights', we are acting specifically *in the name of the Holy Trinity*.

'The most perfect rule of Christianity, its exact

definition, its highest summit, is this: to seek what is for the benefit of all', states St John Chrysostom. '. . . I cannot believe that it is possible for a man to be saved if he does not labour for the salvation of his neighbour.' Such are the practical implications of the dogma of the Trinity. That is what it means to *live the Trinity*.

We glorify not three Gods but one Godhead.
We honour the persons that are truly three,
The Father unbegotten,
The Son begotten from the Father,
The Holy Spirit proceeding from the Father,
One God in three:
And with true faith and glory we ascribe to each
*   the title God.*

From the Lenten Triodion

Come, all peoples, and let us worship the one
*   Godhead in three persons,*
The Son in the Father with the Holy Spirit.
For the Father gave birth outside time to the Son,
Coeternal and enthroned with him;
And the Holy Spirit is glorified in the Father
*   together with the Son:*
One power, one essence, one Godhead,
Whom we all worship, and to whom we say:
Holy God, who hast created all things
Through the Son, by the co-operation of the Holy
*   Spirit;*
Holy and Strong, through whom we know the
*   Father,*
And through whom the Holy Spirit came to dwell
*   within the world;*
Holy and Immortal, Paraclete Spirit,
Proceeding from the Father and resting on the

Son.
Holy Trinity, glory to thee.

From Vespers on the Feast of Pentecost

I praise the Godhead, unity in three persons,
For the Father is light,
The Son is light,
And the Spirit is light.
But the light remains undivided,
Shining forth in oneness of nature,
Yet in the three rays of the persons.

From the Lenten Triodion

Love is the kingdom which the Lord mystically promised to the disciples, when he said that they would eat in his kingdom: 'You shall eat and drink at my table in my kingdom' (Luke 22:30). What should they eat and drink, if not love?

When we have reached love, we have reached God and our journey is complete. We have crossed over to the island which lies beyond the world, where are the Father, the Son and the Holy Spirit: to whom be glory and dominion. May God make us worthy to fear and love him. Amen.

St Isaac the Syrian

However hard I try, I find it impossible to construct anything greater than these three words, 'Love one another' — only to the end, and without exceptions: then all is justified and life is illumined, whereas otherwise it is an abomination and a burden.

Mother Maria of Paris

There can be no Church apart from love.

St John of Kronstadt

Believe me, there is one truth that reigns supreme from the fringes of the throne of glory down to the least shadow of the most insignificant of creatures: and that one truth is love. Love is the source from which the holy streams of grace flow down unceasingly from the city of God, watering the earth and making it fruitful. 'One deep calls to another' (Ps. 42:7): like a deep or an abyss, in its infinity love helps us to picture to ourselves the dread vision of the Godhead. It is love that fashions all things and holds them in unity. It is love that gives life and warmth, that inspires and guides. Love is the seal set upon creation, the signature of the Creator. Love is the explanation of his handiwork.

How can we make Christ come and dwell in our hearts? How else, except through love?

Fr Theoklitos of Dionysiou

Give rest to the weary, visit the sick, support the poor: for this also is prayer.

Aphrahat

The bodies of our fellow human beings must be treated with more care than our own. Christian love teaches us to give our brethren not only spiritual gifts, but material gifts as well. Even our last shirt, our last piece of bread must be given to them. Personal almsgiving and the most wide-ranging social work are equally justifiable and necessary.

The way to God lies through love of other people, and there is no other way. At the Last Judgement I shall not be asked if I was successful in my ascetic exercises or how many prostrations I made in the course of my prayers. I shall be asked, did I feed the hungry, clothe the naked, visit the sick and the

prisoners: that is all I shall be asked.
Mother Maria of Paris

O Trinity supreme in being,
O Unity without beginning,
The hosts of angels sing thy praises, trembling
  before thee.
Heaven, earth and the depths stand in awe of thee,
  all-holy Trinity:
Men bless thee,
Fire is thy servant,
All things created obey thee in fear.
From the Festal Menaion (Mattins on 8 September)

CHAPTER 3

GOD AS CREATOR

*There came to St Antony in the desert one of the wise
men of that time and said: 'Father, how can you
endure to live here, deprived as you are of all consolation from books?' Antony answered: 'My book,
philosopher, is the nature of created things, and
whenever I wish I can read in it the works of God.'*

Evagrius of Pontus

*Understand that you have within yourself, upon a
small scale, a second universe: within you there is a
sun, there is a moon, and there are also stars.*

Origen

Look up to the Heavens

The actress Lillah McCarthy describes how once
she went in great misery to see George Bernard
Shaw, just after she had been deserted by her husband:

*I was shivering. Shaw sat very still. The fire brought
me warmth. . . How long we sat there I do not know,
but presently I found myself walking with dragging
steps with Shaw beside me . . . up and down Adelphi
Terrace. The weight upon me grew a little lighter and
released the tears which would never come before. . .
He let me cry. Presently I heard a voice in which all
the gentleness and tenderness of the world was
speaking. It said: 'Look up, dear, look up to the
heavens. There is more in life than this. There is
much more.'*

Whatever his own faith in God or lack of it, Shaw
points here to something that is fundamental to the

spiritual Way. He did not offer smooth words of consolation to Lillah McCarthy, or pretend that her pain would be easy to bear. What he did was more perceptive. He told her to look out for a moment from herself, from her personal tragedy, and to see the world in its objectivity, to sense its wonder and variety, its 'thusness'. And his advice applies to all of us. However oppressed by my own or others' anguish, I am not to forget that there is more in the world than this, there is much more.

St John of Kronstadt says, 'Prayer is a state of continual gratitude.' If I do not feel a sense of joy in God's creation, if I forget to offer the world back to God with thankfulness, I have advanced very little upon the Way. I have not yet learnt to be truly human. For it is only through thanksgiving that I can *become myself.* Joyful thanksgiving, so far from being escapist or sentimental, is on the contrary entirely realistic — but with the realism of one who *sees the world in God,* as the divine creation.

The Bridge of Diamond

'Thou hast brought us into being out of nothing' (The Liturgy of St John Chrysostom). How are we to understand God's relation to the world he has created? What is meant by this phrase 'out of nothing', *ex nihilo?* Why, indeed, did God create at all?

The words 'out of nothing' signify, first and foremost, that God created the universe *by an act of his free will.* Nothing compelled him to create; he chose to do so. The world was not created unintentionally or out of necessity; it is not an automatic emanation or overflowing from God, but the consequence of divine choice.

If nothing compelled God to create, why then did

he choose to do so? In so far as such a question admits of an answer, our reply must be: God's motive in creation is his love. Rather than say that he created the universe out of nothing, we should say that he created it out of his own self, which is love. We should think, not of God the Manufacturer or God the Craftsman, but of God the Lover. Creation is an act not so much of his free will as of his *free love*. To love means to share, as the doctrine of the Trinity has so clearly shown us: God is not just one but one-in-three, because he is a communion of persons who share in love with one another. The circle of divine love, however, has not remained closed. God's love is, in the literal sense of the word, 'ecstatic' — a love that causes God to go out from himself and to create things other than himself. By voluntary choice God created the world in 'ecstatic' love, so that there might be besides himself other beings to participate in the life and the love that are his.

God was under no compulsion to create; but that does not signify that there was anything incidental or inconsequential about his act of creation. God *is* all that he does, and so his act of creating is not something separate from himself. In God's heart and in his love, each one of us has always existed. From all eternity God saw each one of us as an idea or thought in his divine mind, and for each one from all eternity he has a special and distinctive plan. We have always existed for him; creation signifies that at a certain point in time we begin to exist also for ourselves.

As the fruit of God's free will and free love, the world is not necessary, not self-sufficient, but *contingent* and *dependent*. As created beings we can never be just ourselves alone; God is the core of our being, or we cease to exist. At every moment we depend for our existence upon the loving will of God. Existence is always a *gift* from God — a free gift of his love, a gift that is never taken back, but a gift none the less, not something that we possess by our own power. God alone has the cause and source of his being in himself; all created things have their cause and source, not in themselves, but in him. God alone is self-sourced; all created things are God-sourced, God-rooted, finding their origin and fulfilment in him. God alone is noun; all created things are adjectives.

In saying that God is Creator of the world, we do not mean merely that he set things in motion by an initial act 'at the beginning', after which they go on functioning by themselves. God is not just a cosmic clockmaker, who winds up the machinery and then leaves it to keep ticking on its own. On the contrary, creation is *continual*. If we are to be accurate when speaking of creation, we should use not the past tense but the continuous present. We should say, not 'God made the world, and me in it', but 'God *is making* the world, and me in it, here and now, at this moment and always'. Creation is not an event in the past, but a relationship in the present. If God did not continue to exert his creative will at every moment, the universe would immediately lapse into non-being; nothing could exist for a single second if God did not will it to be. As Metropolitan Philaret of Moscow puts it, 'All creatures are balanced upon the creative word of God, as if upon a bridge of diamond; above them is the abyss of divine infinitude, below them that of their own nothingness.' This is true even of Satan and the fallen angels in hell: they too depend for their existence on the will of God.

The purpose of the creation doctrine, then, is not to ascribe a chronological starting-point to the world, but to affirm that at this present moment, as at all moments, the world depends for its existence upon God. When Genesis states, 'In the beginning God created the heaven and the earth' (1:1), the word 'beginning' is not to be taken simply in a temporal sense, but as signifying that God is the constant cause and sustainer of all things.

As creator, then, God is always at the heart of each thing, maintaining it in being. On the level of scientific inquiry, we discern certain processes or sequences of cause and effect. On the level of spiritual vision, which does not contradict science but looks beyond it, we discern everywhere the creative energies of God, upholding all that is, forming the innermost essence of all things. But, while present everywhere in the world, God is not to be identified with the world. As Christians we affirm not pantheism but 'panentheism'. God is *in* all things yet also *beyond and above* all things. He is both 'greater than the great' and 'smaller than the small'. In the words of St Gregory Palamas, 'He is everywhere and nowhere, he is everything and nothing'. As a Cistercian monk of New Clairvaux has put it, 'God is at the core. God is other than the core. God is within the core, and all through the core, and beyond the core, closer to the core than the core.'

'And God saw every thing that he had made, and, behold, it was exceedingly good' (Gen. 1:31). The creation in its entirety is God's handiwork; in their inner essence all created things are 'exceedingly good'. Christian Orthodoxy repudiates dualism in its various forms: the radical dualism of the Manichaeans, who attribute the existence of evil to a second power, coeternal with the God of love; the less radical dualism of the Gnostic Valentinians, who see the material order, including the human body, as coming into existence in consequence of a pre-cosmic fall; and the more subtle dualism of the Platonists, who regard matter not as evil but as unreal.

Against dualism in all its forms, Christianity affirms that there is a *summum bonum,* a 'supreme good' — namely, God himself — but there is and can be no *summum malum.* Evil is not coeternal with God. In the beginning there was only God: all the things that exist are his creation, whether in heaven or on earth, whether spiritual or physical, and so in their basic 'thusness' they are all of them good.

What, then, are we to say about evil? Since all created things are intrinsically good, sin or evil as such is not a 'thing', not an existent being or substance. 'I did not see sin', says Julian of Norwich in her *Revelations,* 'for I believe that it has no kind of substance, no share in being; nor can it be recognized except by the pain caused by it.' 'Sin is naught', says St Augustine. 'That which is evil in the strict sense', observes Evagrius, 'is not a substance but the absence of good, just as darkness is nothing else than the absence of light.' And St Gregory of Nyssa states, 'Sin does not exist in nature apart from free will; it is not a substance in its own right.' 'Not even the demons are evil by nature', says St Maximus the Confessor, 'but they become such through the misuse of their natural powers.' Evil is always parasitic. It is the twisting and misappropriation of what is in itself good. Evil resides not in the thing itself but in our attitude towards the thing — that is to say, in our will.

It might seem that, by terming evil 'nothing', we are underestimating its forcefulness and dynamism. But, as C.S. Lewis has remarked, Nothing *is* very strong. To say that evil is the perversion of good, and therefore in the final analysis an illusion and unreality, is not to deny its powerful hold over us. For there is no greater force within creation than the free will of beings endowed with self-consciousness and spiritual intellect; and so the misuse of this free will can have altogether terrifying consequences.

Man as Body, Soul and Spirit

And what is man's place in God's creation?

'I pray to God that your whole spirit and soul and body may be preserved blameless until the coming of our Lord Jesus Christ' (1 Thess. 5:23). Here St Paul mentions the three elements or aspects that constitute the human person. While distinct, these aspects are strictly interdependent; man is an integral unity, not the sum total of separable parts.

First, there is the *body,* 'dust from the ground' (Gen. 2:7), the physical or material aspect of man's nature.

Secondly, there is the *soul,* the life-force that vivifies and animates the body, causing it to be not just a lump of matter, but something that grows and moves, that feels and perceives. Animals also possess a soul, and so perhaps do plants. But in man's case the soul is endowed with consciousness; it is a rational soul, possessing the capacity for abstract thought, and the ability to advance by discursive argument from premises to a conclusion. These powers are present in animals, if at all, only to a very limited degree.

Thirdly, there is the *spirit,* the 'breath' from God (see Gen. 2:7), which the animals lack. It is important to distinguish 'Spirit', with an initial capital, from 'spirit' with a small s. The created spirit of man is not to be identified with the uncreated or Holy Spirit of God, the third person of the Trinity; yet the two are intimately connected, for it is through his spirit that man apprehends God and enters into communion with him.

With his soul (*psyche*) man engages in scientific or philosophical inquiry, analysing the data of his sense-experience by means of the discursive reason. With his spirit (*pneuma*), which is sometimes termed *nous* or spiritual intellect, he understands eternal truth about God or about the *logoi* or inner essences of created things, not through deductive reasoning, but by direct apprehension or spiritual perception — by a kind of intuition that St Isaac the Syrian calls 'simple cognition'. The spirit or spiritual intellect is thus distinct from man's reasoning powers and his aesthetic emotions, and superior to both of them.

Because man has a rational soul and a spiritual intellect, he possesses the power of self-determination and of moral freedom, that is to say, the sense of good and evil, and the ability to choose between them. Where the animals act by instinct, man is capable of making a free and conscious decision.

Sometimes the Fathers adopt not a tripartite but a twofold scheme, describing man simply as a unity of body and soul; in that case they treat the spirit or intellect as the highest aspect of the soul. But the threefold scheme of body, soul and spirit is more precise and more illuminating, particularly in our own age when the soul and the spirit are often confused, and when most people are not even aware that they possess a spiritual intellect. The culture and educational system of the contemporary West are based almost exclusively upon the training of the reasoning brain and, to a lesser degree, of the aesthetic emotions. Most of us have forgotten that we are not only brain and will, senses and feelings; we are also spirit. Modern man has for the most part lost touch with the truest and highest aspect of himself; and the result of this inward alienation can be seen all too plainly in his restlessness, his lack of identity and loss of hope.

Microcosm and Mediator

Body, soul and spirit, three in one, man occupies a unique position in the created order.

According to the Orthodox world-view, God has formed two levels of created things: first the 'noetic', 'spiritual' or 'intellectual' level, and secondly, the material or bodily. On the first level God formed the angels, who have no material body. On the second level he formed the physical universe — the galaxies, stars and planets, with the various types of mineral, vegetable and animal life. Man, and man alone, exists on both levels at once. Through his spirit or spiritual intellect he participates in the noetic realm and is a companion of the angels; through his body and his soul, he moves and feels and thinks, he eats and drinks, transmuting food into energy and participating organically in the material realm, which passes within him through his sense-perceptions.

Our human nature is thus more complex than the angelic, and endowed with richer potentialities. Viewed in this perspective, man is not lower but higher than the angels; as the Babylonian Talmud affirms, 'The righteous are greater than the ministering angels' (*Sanhedrin* 93a). Man stands at the heart of God's creation. Participating as he does in both the noetic and the material realms, he is an image or mirror of the whole creation, *imago mundi*, a 'little universe' or microcosm. All created things have their meeting-place in him. Man may say of himself, in the words of Kathleen Raine:

> Because I love
>> The sun pours out its rays of living gold
>> Pours out its gold and silver on the sea...

> Because I love
>> The ferns grow green, and green the grass, and green
>> The transparent sunlit trees...

> Because I love
>> All night the river flows into my sleep,
>> Ten thousand living things are sleeping in my arms,
>> And sleeping wake, and flowing are at rest.

Being microcosm, man is also mediator. It is his God-given task to reconcile and harmonize the noetic and the material realms, to bring them to unity, to spiritualize the material, and to render manifest all the latent capacities of the created order. As the Jewish Hasidim expressed it, man is called 'to advance from rung to rung until, through him, everything is united'. As microcosm, then, man is the one in whom the world is summed up; as mediator, he is the one through whom the world is offered back to God.

Man is able to exercise this mediating role only because his human nature is essentially and fundamentally a unity. If he were just a soul dwelling temporarily in a body, as many of the Greek and Indian philosophers have imagined — if his body were no part of his true self, but only a piece of clothing which he will eventually lay aside, or a prison from which he is seeking to escape — then man could not properly act as mediator. Man spiritualizes the creation first of all by spiritualizing his own body and offering it to God. 'Do you not realize that your body is a temple of the Holy Spirit that is in you?' writes St Paul. '. . . Glorify God with your body . . . I beseech you therefore, brethren, by the mercies of God, that you offer your bodies as a living sacrifice, holy, acceptable to God' (1 Cor. 6:19-20; Rom. 12:1). But in 'spiritualizing' the body, man does not thereby dematerialize it: on the contrary, it is the human vocation to manifest the spiritual *in and through the material*. Christians are in this sense the only true materialists.

The body, then, is an integral part of human personhood. The separation of body and soul at death is *un*natural, something contrary to God's original plan, that has come about in consequence of the fall. Furthermore, the separation is only temporary: we look forward, beyond death, to the final resurrection on the Last Day, when body and soul will be reunited once again.

Image and Likeness

'The glory of God is man', affirms the Talmud (*Derech Eretz Zutta* 10,5); and St Irenaeus states the same: 'The glory of God is a living man.' The human person forms the centre and crown of God's creation. Man's unique position in the cosmos is indicated above all by the fact that he is made 'in the image and likeness' of God (Gen. 1:26). Man is a finite expression of God's infinite self-expression.

Sometimes the Greek Fathers associate the divine image or 'ikon' in man with the totality of his nature, considered as a triunity of spirit, soul and body. At other times they connect the image more specifically with the highest aspect of man, with his spirit or spiritual intellect, through which he attains knowledge of God and union with him. Fundamentally, the image of God in man denotes everything that distinguishes man from the animals, that makes him in the full and true sense a *person* — a moral agent capable of right and wrong, a spiritual subject endowed with inward freedom.

The aspect of *free choice* is particularly important for an understanding of man as made in God's image. As God is free, so likewise man is free. And, being free, each human being realizes the divine image within himself in his own distinctive fashion. Human beings are not counters that can be exchanged for one another, or replaceable parts of a machine. Each, being free, is unrepeatable; and each, being unrepeatable, is infinitely precious. Human persons are not to be measured quantitatively: we have no right to assume that one particular person is of more value than any other particular person, or that ten persons must necessarily be of more value than one. Such calculations are an offence to authentic personhood. Each is irreplaceable, and therefore each must be treated as an *end* in his or her self, and never as a means to some further end. Each is to be regarded not as object but as subject. If we find people boring and tediously predictable, that is because we have not broken through to the level of true personhood, in others and in ourselves, where there are no stereotypes but each is unique.

By many of the Greek Fathers, although not by all, a distinction is drawn between the 'image' of God and the 'likeness' of God. The image, for those who distinguish the two terms, denotes man's *potentiality* for life in God, the likeness his *realization* of that potentiality. The image is that which man possesses from the beginning, and which enables him to set out in the first place upon the spiritual Way; the likeness is that which he hopes to attain at his journey's end. In the words of Origen, 'Man received the honour of the image at his first creation, but the full perfection of God's likeness will only be conferred upon him at the consummation of all things.' All men are made in the image of God and, however corrupt their lives may be, the divine image within them is merely obscured and crusted over, yet never altogether lost. But the likeness is fully achieved only by the blessed in the heavenly kingdom of the Age to come.

According to St Irenaeus, man at his first creation was 'as a little child', and needed to 'grow' into his perfection. In other words, man at his first creation was innocent and capable of developing spiritually (the 'image'), but this development was not inevitable or automatic. Man was called to cooperate with God's grace and so, through the correct use of his free will, slowly and by gradual steps he was to become perfect in God (the 'likeness'). This shows how the notion of man as created in God's image can be interpreted in a dynamic rather than a static sense. It need not mean that man was endowed from the outset with a fully realized perfection, with the highest possible holiness and knowledge, but simply that he was given the *opportunity to grow* into full fellowship with God. The image-likeness distinction does not, of course, in itself imply the acceptance of any 'theory of evolution'; but it is not incompatible with such a theory.

The image and likeness signify orientation, relationship. As Philip Sherrard observes, 'The very concept of man implies a relationship, a connection with God. Where one affirms man one also affirms God.' To believe that man is made in God's image is to believe that man is created for communion and union with God, and that if he rejects this communion he ceases to be properly man. There is no such thing as 'natural man' existing in separation from God: man cut off from God is in a highly *un*natural state. The image doctrine means, therefore, that man has God as the innermost centre of his being. The divine is the determining element in our humanity; losing our sense of the divine, we lose also our sense of the human.

This is strikingly confirmed by what has happened in the West since the Renaissance, and more notably since the industrial revolution. An increasing secularism has been accompanied by a growing dehumanization of society. The clearest example of this is to be seen in the Leninist-Stalinist version of Communism, as found in the Soviet Union. Here the denial of God has gone hand in hand with a cruel repression of man's personal freedom. Nor is this in the least surprising. The only secure basis for a doctrine of human liberty and human dignity is the belief that each man is in God's image.

Man is made, not only in the image of God, but more specifically in the image of *God the Trinity*. All that was said earlier about 'living the Trinity' (pp. 48–50) acquires added force when spelt out in terms of the image doctrine. Since the image of God in man is a Trinitarian image, it follows that man, like God, realizes his true nature through mutual life. The image signifies relationship not only with God but with other men. Just as the three divine persons live in and for each other, so man — being made in the Trinitarian image — becomes a real person by seeing the world through others' eyes, by making others' joys and sorrows his own. Each human being is unique, yet each in uniqueness is created for communion with others.

'We who are of the faith should look on all the faithful as but a single person . . . and should be ready to lay down our lives for the sake of our neighbour' (St Symeon the New Theologian). 'There is no other way to be saved, except through our neighbour. . . This is purity of heart: when you see the sinful or the sick, to feel compassion for them and to be tenderhearted towards them' (*The Homilies of St Macarius*). 'The old men used to say that we should each of us look upon our neighbour's experiences as if they were our own. We should suffer with our neighbour in everything and weep with him, and should behave as if we were inside his body; and if any trouble befalls him, we should feel as much distress as we would for ourselves' (*The Sayings of the Desert Fathers*). All this is true, precisely because man is made in the image of God the Trinity.

Priest and King

Made in the divine image, microcosm and mediator, man is priest and king of the creation. Consciously and with deliberate purpose, he can do two things that the animals can only do unconsciously and instinctively. First, man is able to *bless and praise God for the world*. Man is best defined not as a 'logical' but as a 'eucharistic' animal. He does not merely live in the world, think about it and use it, but he is capable of seeing the world as God's gift, as a sacrament of God's presence and a means of communion with him. So he is able to offer the world back to God in thanksgiving: 'Thine own from thine own we offer to thee, in all and for all' (The Liturgy of St John Chrysostom).

Secondly, besides blessing and praising God for the world, man is also able to *reshape and alter the world,* and so to endue it with fresh meaning. In the words of Fr Dumitru Staniloae, 'Man puts the seal of his understanding and of his intelligent work onto creation. . . The world is not only a gift, but a task for man.' It is our calling to co-operate with God; we are, in St Paul's phrase, 'fellow-workers with God' (1 Cor. 3:9). Man is not just a logical and eucharistic animal, but he is also a creative animal: the fact that man is in God's image means that man is a creator after the image of God the Creator. This creative role he fulfils, not by brute force, but through the clarity of his spiritual vision; his vocation is not to dominate and exploit nature, but to transfigure and hallow it.

In a variety of ways — through the cultivation of the earth, through craftsmanship, through the writing of books and the painting of ikons — man gives material things a voice and renders the creation articulate in praise of God. It is significant that the first task of the newly-created Adam was to give names to the animals (Gen. 2:19-20). The giving of names is in itself a creative act: until we have found a name for some object or experience, an 'inevitable word' to indicate its true character, we cannot begin to understand it and to make use of it. It is likewise significant that, when at the Eucharist we offer back to God the firstfruits of the earth, we offer them not in their original form but reshaped by the hand of man: we bring to the altar not sheaves of wheat but loaves of bread, not grapes but wine.

So man is priest of the creation through his power to give thanks and to offer the creation back to God; and he is king of the creation through his power to mould and fashion, to connect and diversify. This hieratic and royal function is beautifully described by St Leontius of Cyprus:

Through heaven and earth and sea, through wood and stone, through all creation visible and invisible, I offer veneration to the Creator and Master and Maker of all things. For the creation does not venerate the Maker directly and by itself, but it is through me that the heavens declare the glory of God, through me the moon worships God, through me the stars glorify him, through me the waters and showers of rain, the dews and all creation, venerate God and give him glory.

Similar ideas are expressed by the Hasidic master Abraham Yaakov of Sadagora:

All creatures and plants and animals bring and offer themselves to man, but through man they are all brought and offered to God. When man purifies and sanctifies himself in all his members as an offering to God, he purifies and sanctifies all the creatures.

The Inner Kingdom

'Blessed are the pure in heart, for they shall see God' (Matt. 5:8). Made in God's image, man is a mirror of the divine. He knows God by knowing himself: entering within himself, he sees God reflected in the purity of his own heart. The doctrine of man's creation according to the image means that within each person — within his or her truest and innermost self, often termed the 'deep heart' or 'ground of the soul' — there is a point of direct meeting and union with the Uncreated. 'The kingdom of God is within you' (Luke 17:21).

This quest for the inward kingdom is one of the master themes found throughout the writings of the Fathers. 'The greatest of all lessons', says St Clement of Alexandria, 'is to know oneself; for if someone knows himself, he will know God; and if he knows God, he will become like God.' St Basil the Great writes: 'When the intellect is no longer dissipated among external things or dispersed across the world through the senses, it returns to itself; and by means of itself it ascends to the thought of God.' 'He who knows himself knows everything', says St Isaac the Syrian; and elsewhere he writes:

Be at peace with your own soul; then heaven and earth will be at peace with you. Enter eagerly into the treasure house that is within you, and so you will see the things that are in heaven; for there is but one single entry to them both. The ladder that leads to the kingdom is hidden within your soul. Flee from sin, dive into yourself, and in your soul you will discover the stairs by which to ascend.

And to these passages we may add the testimony of a Western witness in our own day, Thomas Merton:

At the centre of our being is a point of nothingness which is untouched by sin and by illusion, a point of pure truth, a point or spark which belongs entirely to God, which is never at our disposal, from which God disposes of our lives, which is inaccessible to the fantasies of our own mind or the brutalities of our own will. This little point of nothingness and of absolute poverty is the pure glory of God in us. It is

*so to speak his name written in us, as our poverty, as
our indigence, as our.dependence, as our sonship.
It is like a pure diamond, blazing with the invisible
light of heaven. It is in everybody, and if we could
see it we would see these billions of points of light
coming together in the face and blaze of a sun that
would make all the darkness and cruelty of life
vanish completely. . . The gate of heaven is everywhere.*

Flee from sin, St Isaac insists; and these three
words should be particularly noted. If we are to see
God's face reflected within us, the mirror needs to
be cleaned. Without repentance there can be no
self-knowledge and no discovery of the inward kingdom. When I am told, 'Return into yourself: know
yourself', it is necessary to inquire: Which 'self' am I
to discover? What *is* my true self? Psychoanalysis
discloses to us one type of 'self'; all too often,
however, it guides us, not to the 'ladder that leads
to the kingdom', but to the staircase that goes down
to a dank and snake-infested cellar. 'Know yourself' means 'know yourself as God-sourced, God-
rooted; know yourself in God'. From the viewpoint
of the Orthodox spiritual tradition it should be
emphasized that we shall not discover this, our true
self 'according to the image', except through a death
to our false and fallen self. 'He who loses his life for
my sake shall find it' (Matt. 16:25): only the one
who sees his false self for what it is and rejects it,
will be able to discern his true self, the self that God
sees. Underlining this distinction between the false
self and the true, St Varsanuphius enjoins: 'Forget
yourself and know yourself.'

Evil, Suffering, and the Fall of Man

In Dostoevsky's greatest novel, *The Brothers Karamazov,* Ivan challenges his brother: 'Suppose that you are creating the fabric of human destiny with the object of making people happy at last and giving them peace and rest, but that in order to do so it is necessary to torture a single tiny baby . . . and to found your building on its tears— would you agree to undertake the building on that condition?' 'No, I wouldn't agree', answers Alyosha. And if we wouldn't agree to do this, then why apparently does God?

Somerset Maugham tells us that, after seeing a small child slowly die from meningitis, he could no longer believe in a God of love. Others have had to watch a husband or wife, a child or parent, lapse into total depression: in the whole realm of suffering there is perhaps nothing so terrible to contemplate as a human being with chronic melancholia. What is our anwer? How are we to reconcile faith in a loving God, who created all things and saw that they were 'exceedingly good', with the existence of pain, sin and evil?

At once it must be admitted that no easy answer or obvious reconciliation is possible. Pain and evil confront us as a surd. Suffering, our own and that of others, is an experience through which we have to live, not a theoretical problem that we can explain away. If there is an explanation, it is on a level deeper than words. Suffering cannot be 'justified'; but it can be used, accepted — and, through this acceptance, transfigured. 'The paradox of suffering and evil', says Nicolas Berdyaev, 'is resolved in the experience of compassion and love.'

But, while we are rightly suspicious of any facile

resolution of the 'problem of evil', we can find in the account of man's fall, given in the third chapter of Genesis — whether this be interpreted literally or symbolically — two vital signposts, to be read with care.

First, the Genesis account begins by speaking of the 'serpent' (3:1), that is to say, the devil — the first among those angels who turned away from God to the hell of self-will. There has been a double fall: first of the angels, and then of man. For Orthodoxy the fall of the angels is not a picturesque fairy-tale but spiritual truth. Prior to man's creation, there had already occurred a parting of the ways within the noetic realm: some of the angels remained steadfast in obedience to God, others rejected him. Concerning this 'war in heaven' (Rev. 12:7) we have only cryptic references in Scripture; we are not told in detail what happened, still less do we know what plans God has for a possible reconciliation within the noetic realm, or how (if at all) the devil may eventually be redeemed. Perhaps, as the first chapter of the Book of Job suggests, Satan is not as black as he is usually painted. For us, at this present stage in our earthly existence, Satan is the enemy; but Satan has also a direct relationship with God, of which we know nothing at all and about which it is not wise for us to speculate. Let us mind our own business.

Three points, however, should be noted which do concern us in our efforts to come to grips with the problem of pain. First, besides the evil for which we humans are personally responsible, there are present in the universe forces of immense potency whose will is turned to evil. These forces, while non-human, are nevertheless personal. The existence of such demonic powers is not a hypothesis or legend but — for very many of us, alas! — a matter of direct experience. Secondly, the existence of fallen spiritual powers helps us to understand why, at a point in time apparently prior to man's creation, there should be found in the world of nature disorder, waste and cruelty. Thirdly, the rebellion of the angels makes it abundantly clear that evil originates not from below but from above, not from matter but from spirit. Evil, as already emphasized, is 'no thing' (see p. 59); it is not an existent being or substance, but a wrong attitude towards what in itself is good. The source of evil lies thus in the *free will* of spiritual beings endowed with moral choice, who use that power of choice incorrectly.

So much for our first signpost, the allusion to the 'serpent'. But (and this may serve as our second signpost) the Genesis account makes it clear that, although man comes into existence in a world already tainted by the fall of the angels, yet at the same time nothing compelled man to sin. Eve was tempted by the 'serpent', but she was free to reject his suggestions. Her and Adam's 'original sin' consisted in a *conscious* act of disobedience, a *deliberate* rejection of God's love, a *freely-chosen* turning from God to self (Gen. 3:2,3,11).

In man's possession and exercise of free will we find, by no means a complete explanation, but at least the beginnings of an answer to our problem. Why has God allowed the angels and man to sin? Why does God permit evil and suffering? We answer: Because he is a God of love. Love implies sharing, and love also implies freedom. As a Trinity of love, God desired to share his life with created persons made in his image, who would be capable of responding to him freely and willingly in a relationship of love. *Where there is no freedom, there can be no love.* Compulsion excludes love; as Paul Evdokimov used to say, God can do everything except compel us to love him. God, therefore — desiring to share his love — created, not robots who would obey him mechanically, but angels and human beings endowed with free choice. And thereby, to put the matter in an anthropomorphic way, God took a risk: for with this gift of freedom there was given also the possibility of sin. But he who takes no risks does not love.

Without freedom there would be no sin. But without freedom man would not be in God's image; without freedom man would not be capable of entering into communion with God in a relationship of love.

Consequences of the Fall

Created for fellowship with the Holy Trinity, called to advance in love from the divine image to the divine likeness, man chose instead a path that led not up but down. He repudiated the Godward relationship that is his true essence. Instead of acting as mediator and unifying centre, he produced division: division within himself, division between himself and other men, division between himself and the world of nature. Entrusted by God with the gift of freedom, he systematically denied freedom to his fellows. Blessed with the power to reshape the world and to endue it with fresh meaning, he misused that power in order to fashion instruments of ugliness and destruction. The consequences of this misuse, more particularly since the industrial revolution, have now become hideously apparent in the rapid pollution of the environment.

The 'original sin' of man, his turning from God-centredness to self-centredness, meant first and foremost that he no longer looked upon the world and other human beings in a eucharistic way, as a sacrament of communion with God. He ceased to regard them as a gift, to be offered back in thanksgiving to the Giver, and he began to treat them as his own possession, to be grasped, exploited and devoured. So he no longer saw other persons and things as they are in themselves and in God, and he saw them only in terms of the pleasure and satisfaction which they could give to him. And the result of this was that he was caught in the vicious circle of his own lust, which grew more hungry the more it was gratified. The world ceased to be transparent —a window through which he gazed on God —and it grew opaque; it ceased to be life-giving, and became subject to corruption and mortality. 'For dust thou art, and unto dust shalt thou return' (Gen. 3:19). This is true of fallen man and of every created thing, so soon as it is cut off from the one source of life, God himself.

The effects of man's fall were both physical and moral. On the physical level human beings became subject to pain and disease, to the debility and bodily disintegration of old age. Woman's joy in bringing forth new life became mixed with the pangs of childbirth (Gen. 3:16). None of this was part of God's initial plan for humanity. In consequence of the fall, men and women also became subject to the separation of soul and body in physical death. Yet physical death should be seen, not primarily as a punishment, but as a means of release provided by a loving God. In his mercy God did not wish men to go on living indefinitely in a fallen world, caught for ever in the vicious circle of their own devising; and so he provided a way of escape. For death is not the end of life but the beginning of its renewal. We look, beyond physical death, to the future reunion of body and soul at the general resurrection on the Last Day. In separating our body and soul at death, therefore, God is acting like the potter: when the vessel upon his wheel has become marred and twisted, he breaks the clay in pieces so as to fashion it anew (compare Jer. 18:1-6). This is emphasized in the Orthodox funeral service:

Of old thou hast created me from nothing,
And honoured me with thy divine image;
But when I disobeyed thy commandment,
Thou hast returned me to the earth whence I was
taken.
Lead me back again to thy likeness,
Refashioning my ancient beauty.

On the moral level, in consequence of the fall human beings became subject to frustration, boredom, depression. Work, which was intended to be a source of joy for man and a means of communion with God, had now to be performed for the most part unwillingly, 'in the sweat of the face' (Gen. 3:19). Nor was this all. Man became subject to inward alienation: weakened in will, divided against himself, he became his own enemy and executioner. As St Paul puts it, 'I know that in me (that is, in my flesh) dwells nothing good. I am able to choose with my will, but how I am actually to carry out what is good I do not know. For the good which I choose I do not do; but the evil which I do not choose, that I do . . . O wretched man that I am! Who will deliver me?' (Rom. 7:18,19,24). Here St Paul is not just saying that there is a conflict within us between good and evil. He is saying that, all too often, we find ourselves morally paralysed: we sincerely desire to choose the good, but we find ourselves caught in a situation where *all* our choices result in evil. And each of us knows from personal experience exactly what St Paul means.

St Paul, however, is careful to say: 'I know that in my *flesh* dwells nothing good'. Our ascetic warfare is against the flesh, not against the body as such. 'Flesh' is not the same as 'body'. The term flesh, as used in the passage just quoted, signifies whatever within us is sinful and opposed to God; thus it is not only the body but the soul in fallen man that has become fleshly and carnal. We are to hate the flesh, but we are not to hate the body, which is God's handiwork and the temple of the Holy Spirit. Ascetic self-denial is thus a fight against the flesh, but it is a fight not against but *for* the body. As Fr Sergei Bulgakov used to say, 'Kill the flesh, in order to acquire a body.' Asceticism is not self-enslavement, but the way to freedom. Man is a tangled mesh of self-contradictions: only through asceticism can he gain spontaneity.

Asceticism, understood in this sense as a struggle against the flesh, against the sinful and fallen aspect of the self, is clearly something that is required from *all* Christians, and not only from those under monastic vows. The monastic vocation and that of marriage — the way of negation and the way of affirmation — are to be seen as parallel and complementary. The monk or nun is not a dualist but, to the same degree as the married Christian, is seeking to proclaim the intrinsic goodness of the material creation and of the human body; and, by the same token, the married Christian is called to asceticism. The difference lies solely in the outward conditions under which the ascetic warfare is carried on. Both alike are ascetics, both alike are materialists (using the word in its true Christian sense). Both alike are sin-denying and world-affirming.

The Orthodox tradition, without minimizing the effects of the fall, does not however believe that it resulted in a 'total depravity', such as the Calvinists assert in their more pessimistic moments. The divine image in man was obscured but not oblite-rated. His free choice has been restricted in its exercise but not destroyed. Even in a fallen world man is still capable of generous self-sacrifice and loving compassion. Even in a fallen world man still retains some knowledge of God and can enter by grace into communion with him. There are many saints in the pages of the Old Testament, men and women such as Abraham and Sarah, Joseph and Moses, Elijah and Jeremiah; and outside the Chosen People of Israel there are figures such as Socrates who not only taught the truth but lived it. Yet it remains true that human sin — the original sin of Adam, compounded by the personal sins of each succeeding generation — has set a gulf between God and man such that man by his own efforts could not bridge.

No one falls alone

For the Orthodox tradition, then, Adam's origi-nal sin affects the human race in its entirety, and it has consequences both on the physical and the moral level: it results not only in sickness and physical death, but in moral weakness and paraly-sis. But does it also imply an inherited *guilt*? Here Orthodoxy is more guarded. Original sin is not to be interpreted in juridical or quasi-biological terms, as if it were some physical 'taint' of guilt, transmitted through sexual intercourse. This picture, which normally passes for the Augustinian view, is unacceptable to Orthodoxy. The doctrine of original sin means rather that we are born into an environment where it is easy to do evil and hard to do good; easy to hurt others, and hard to heal their wounds; easy to arouse men's suspicions, and hard to win their trust. It means that we are each of us conditioned by the solidarity of the human race in its accumulated wrong-doing and wrong-thinking, and hence wrong-being. And to this accumulation of wrong we have ourselves added by our own deliberate acts of sin. The gulf grows wider and wider.

It is here, in the solidarity of the human race, that we find an explanation for the apparent unjustness of the doctrine of original sin. Why, we ask, should the entire human race suffer because of Adam's fall? Why should all be punished because of one man's sin? The answer is that human beings, made in the image of the Trinitarian God, are interdependent and coinherent. No man is an island. We are 'members one of another'(Eph. 4:25), and so any action, performed by any member of the human race, inevitably affects all the other members. Even though we are not, in the strict sense, *guilty* of the sins of others, yet we are somehow always *involved*.

'When anyone falls', states Aleksei Khomiakov, 'he falls alone; but no one is saved alone.' Should he not have said also that no one falls alone? Dostoevsky's *Starets* Zosima in *The Brothers Karamazov* comes closer to the truth when he says that we are each of us 'responsible for everyone and everything':

There is only one way to salvation, and that is to

make yourself responsible for all men's sins. As soon as you make yourself responsible in all sincerity for everything and for everyone, you will see at once that this is really so, and that you are in fact to blame for everyone and for all things.

A Suffering God?

Does our sin cause sorrow to the heart of God? Does he suffer when we suffer? Do we have the right to say to the man or woman who is suffering: 'God himself, *at this very moment,* is suffering what you suffer, and is overcoming it'?

Wishing to safeguard the divine transcendence, the early Fathers, Greek and Latin, insisted upon the 'impassibility' of God. Strictly interpreted, this means that, while God-made-man can and does suffer, God in himself does not. Without denying the Patristic teaching, should we not also say something more than this? In the Old Testament, long before Christ's Incarnation, we find it stated of God: 'His soul was grieved for the misery of Israel' (Judg. 10:16). Elsewhere in the Old Testament words such as these are put into God's mouth: 'Is Ephraim my dear son? Is he my beloved child? For though I turned my back on him, yet do I earnestly remember him still; therefore my heart is troubled for him' (Jer. 31:20). 'How can I give thee up, Ephraim? How shall I abandon thee, Israel? My heart is moved within me' (Hos. 11:8).

If these passages mean anything at all, they must mean that even before the Incarnation God is directly involved in the sufferings of his creation. Our misery causes grief to God; the tears of God are joined to those of man. A proper respect for the apophatic approach will, of course, make us wary of ascribing human feelings to God in a crude or unqualified way. But this at least we are entitled to affirm. 'Love makes others' sufferings its own', states *The Book of the Poor in Spirit*. If this is true of human love, it is much more true of divine love. Since God is love and created the world as an act of love — and since God is personal, and personhood implies sharing — God does not remain indifferent to the sorrows of this fallen world. If I as a human being remain unaffected by another's anguish, in what sense do I genuinely love him? Surely, then, God identifies himself with his creation in its anguish.

It has been truly said that there was a cross in the heart of God before there was one planted outside Jerusalem; and though the cross of wood has been taken down, the cross in God's heart still remains. It is the cross of pain and triumph — both together. And those who can believe this will find that joy is mingled with their cup of bitterness. They will share on a human level in the divine experience of victorious suffering.

───────

O thou who coverest thy high places with the
 waters,
Who settest the sand as a bound to the sea
And dost uphold all things:
The sun sings thy praises,
The moon gives thee glory,
Every creature offers a hymn to thee,
His author and creator, for ever.
      From the Lenten Triodion

84

Great art thou, O Lord, and marvellous are thy works: no words suffice to sing the praise of thy wonders.

For thou by thine own will hast brought all things out of nothingness into being: by thy power thou dost hold together the creation and by thy providence thou dost govern the world.

Of four elements hast thou compounded the creation: with four seasons hast thou crowned the circuit of the year.

All the spiritual powers tremble before thee.

The sun sings thy praises;

The moon glorifies thee;

The stars supplicate before thee;

The light obeys thee;

The deeps are afraid at thy presence;

The fountains are thy servants.

Thou hast stretched out the heavens like a curtain;

Thou hast established the earth upon the waters;

Thou hast walled about the sea with sand.

Thou has poured forth the air that living things may breathe.

The angelic powers minister to thee; the choirs of archangels worship thee; the many-eyed cherubim and the six-winged seraphim, standing round thee and flying about thee, hide their faces in fear of thine unapproachable glory. . .

By the elements, by the angels and by men, by things visible and invisible, may thy most holy name be glorified, together with the Father and the Holy Spirit, now and ever, and to the ages of ages. Amen.

Prayer at the Great Blessing of the Waters
(Feast of Epiphany)

The divine risk, inherent in the decision to create beings in the image and likeness of God, is the summit of almighty power, or rather a surpassing of that summit in voluntarily undertaken powerlessness. For 'the weakness of God is stronger than men' (1 Cor. 1:25).

Vladimir Lossky

The universe is the vineyard given to men by God. 'All things are for our sake, not we for theirs', says St John Chrysostom. Everything is God's gift to man, a sign of his love. All things bear witness to the sap of God's love, his good will or grace, and communicate it to us. Consequently everything is a vehicle of this divine gift of love, just as every gift that we make to one another is a sign and vehicle of love for each other. But a gift calls for a responding gift, so that the reciprocity of love may be realized. To God, however, man can give back nothing but what has been given him for his needs; his gift, therefore, is sacrifice and he offers it in thanksgiving to God. Man's gift to God is sacrifice and 'eucharist' in the widest sense.

Yet in offering the world to God as a gift or sacrifice, we set on it the seal of our own work, of our understanding, of our spirit of sacrifice, of our own movement towards God. The more we grasp the value and complexity of this divine gift and develop its potentialities, and thereby increase the talents that have been given us, the more we praise God and give him joy, proving that we are active partners in the dialogue of love between him and us.

Fr Dumitru Staniloae

In the immense cathedral which is the universe of God, each man, whether scholar or manual labourer, is called to act as the priest of his whole life — to take all that is human, and to turn it into an offering and a hymn of glory.

Paul Evdokimov

If a few men become prayer — prayer that is 'pure' and to all appearances quite useless — they transform the universe by the sole fact of their presence, by their very existence.

Olivier Clément

You are a world within a world: look within yourself, and see there the whole creation. Do not look at exterior things but turn all your attention to that which lies within. Gather together your whole mind within the intellectual treasure-house of your soul, and make ready for the Lord a shrine free from images.

St Nilus of Ancyra

It seems to the Russian that man can know a thing, as man, only through participation.

Good and evil are, here on earth, inextricably bound up together. This is, to us, the great mystery of life on earth. Where evil is at its most intense, there too must be the greatest good. To us this is not even an hypothesis. It is axiomatic.

Evil must not be shunned, but first participated in and understood through participation, and then through understanding redeemed and transfigured.

Iulia de Beausobre

The saints must needs offer repentance not only on their own behalf but also on behalf of their neighbour, for without active love they cannot be made perfect. So the whole universe is held together, and we are each of us helped providentially by one an-

other.

St Mark the Monk

God does not insist or desire that we should mourn in agony of heart; rather, it is his wish that out of love for him we should rejoice with laughter in our soul. Take away sin, and tears become superfluous; where there is no bruise, no ointment is required. Before the fall Adam shed no tears, and in the same way there will be no more tears after the resurrection from the dead, when sin has been destroyed. For pain, sorrow and lamentation will then have fled away.

St John Climacus

The glory to which man is called is that he should grow more godlike by growing ever more human.

Fr Dumitru Staniloae

CHAPTER 4

GOD AS MAN

God was in Christ, reconciling the world unto himself.

2 Corinthians 5:19

Thirst after Jesus, and he will satisfy you with his love.

St Isaac the Syrian

Abba Isaac said: 'Once I was sitting with Abba Poemen, and I saw that he was in an ecstasy; and since I used to speak very openly with him, I made a prostration before him and asked him, "Tell me, where were you?" And he did not want to tell me. But when I pressed him, he replied: "My thoughts were with St Mary the Mother of God, as she stood and wept at the Cross of the Saviour; and I wish that I could always weep as much as she wept then." '

The Sayings of the Desert Fathers

Our Companion on the Way

Towards the end of *The Waste Land* T. S. Eliot writes:

Who is the third who walks always beside you?
When I count, there are only you and I together
But when I look ahead up the white road
There is always another one walking beside you. . .

He explains in the notes that he has in mind the story told of Shackleton's Antarctic expedition:

how the party of explorers, when at the extremity of their strength, repeatedly felt that there was *one more member* than could actually be counted. Long before Shackleton, King Nebuchadnezzar of Babylon had a similar experience: 'Did we not cast three men bound into the midst of the fire? Yet I see four men loose, walking in the midst of the fire, and they have no hurt; and the form of the fourth is like the Son of God' (Dan. 3:24-25).

Such is for us the meaning of Jesus our Saviour. He is the one who walks always beside us when we are at the extremity of our strength, who is with us in the wilderness of ice or in the furnace of fire. To each of us, at the time of our greatest loneliness or trial, this word is said: *You are not alone*; you have a companion.

We ended our last chapter by speaking of man's alienation and exile. We saw how sin, original and personal, has set between God and man a gulf which man by his own unaided efforts cannot bridge. Cut off from his Creator, separated from his fellow men, inwardly fragmented, fallen man lacked the power to heal himself. Where, so we asked, was a cure to be found? We saw also how the Trinity, as a God of personal love, could not remain indifferent to man's suffering, but was involved in it. How far has this divine involvement been carried?

The answer is that it has been carried to the furthest possible extent. Since man could not come to God, God has come to man, identifying himself with man in the most direct way. The eternal Logos and Son of God, the second person of the Trinity, has become true man, one of us; he has healed and restored our manhood by taking the whole of it into himself. In the words of the Creed: 'I believe . . . in one Lord Jesus Christ . . . true God from true God, one in essence with the Father . . . who for us men and for our salvation came down from heaven, and was incarnate by the Holy Spirit from the Virgin Mary. . .' This, then, is our companion in the ice or the fire: the Lord Jesus who took flesh from the Virgin, one of the Trinity yet one of us, our God yet our brother.

Lord Jesus, have mercy

In an earlier section (p. 48), we explored the Trinitarian meaning of the Jesus Prayer, 'Lord Jesus Christ, Son of God, have mercy on me a sinner'. Let us now consider what it has to tell us about the Incarnation of Jesus Christ, and about our healing by and in him.

There are in the Jesus Prayer two 'poles' or extreme points. 'Lord . . . Son of God': the Prayer speaks first about God's glory, acclaiming Jesus as the Lord of all creation and the eternal Son. Then at its conclusion the Prayer turns to our condition as sinners — sinful by virtue of the fall, sinful through our personal acts of wrongdoing: '. . . on me a sinner'. (In its literal meaning the Greek text is yet more emphatic, saying 'on me *the* sinner', as if I were the only one.)

So the Prayer begins with adoration and ends with penitence. Who or what is to reconcile these two extremes of divine glory and human sinfulness? There are three words in the Prayer which give the answer. The first is 'Jesus', the personal name conferred on Christ after his human birth from the Virgin Mary. This has the sense of *Saviour*: as the angel said to Christ's foster-father St Joseph: 'You shall call his name Jesus, for he shall save his people from their sins' (Matt. 1:21).

The second word is the title 'Christ', the Greek equivalent of the Hebrew 'Messiah', meaning the *Anointed One* — anointed, that is, by the Holy Spirit of God. For the Jewish people of the Old Covenant, the Messiah was the coming deliverer, the future king, who in the power of the Spirit would set them free from their enemies.

The third word is 'mercy', a term that signifies *love in action,* love working to bring about forgiveness, liberation and wholeness. To have mercy is to acquit the other of the guilt which by his own efforts he cannot wipe away, to release him from the debts he himself cannot pay, to make him whole from the sickness for which he cannot unaided find any cure. The term 'mercy' means furthermore that all this is conferred as a free gift: the one who asks for mercy has no claims upon the other, no rights to which he can appeal.

The Jesus Prayer, then, indicates both man's problem and God's solution. Jesus is the Saviour, the anointed king, the one who has mercy. But the Prayer also tells us something more about the person of Jesus himself. He is addressed as 'Lord' and 'Son of God': here the Prayer speaks of his Godhead, of his transcendence and eternity. But he is addressed equally as 'Jesus', that is, by the personal name which his mother and his foster-father gave him after his human birth in Bethlehem. So the Prayer speaks also of his manhood, of the genuine reality of his birth as a human being.

The Jesus Prayer is thus an affirmation of faith in Jesus Christ as alike truly divine and fully human. He is the *Theanthropos* or 'God-man', who saves us from our sins precisely because he is God and man at once. Man could not come to God, so God has come to man — by making himself human. In his outgoing or 'ecstatic' love, God unites himself to his creation in the closest of all possible unions, by himself becoming that which he has created. God, as man, fulfils the mediatorial task which man rejected at the fall. Jesus our Saviour bridges the abyss between God and man because he is both at once. As we say in one of the Orthodox hymns for Christmas Eve, 'Heaven and earth are united today, for Christ is born. Today has God come down to earth, and man gone up to heaven.'

The Incarnation, then, is God's supreme act of deliverance, restoring us to communion with himself. But what would have happened if there had never been a fall? Would God have chosen to become man, even if man had never sinned? Should the Incarnation be regarded simply as God's response to the predicament of fallen man, or is it in some way part of the eternal purpose of God? Should we look behind the fall, and see God's act of becoming man as the fulfilment of man's true destiny?

To this hypothetical question it is not possible for us, in our present situation, to give any final answer. Living as we do under the conditions of the fall, we cannot clearly imagine what God's relation to mankind would have been, had the fall never occurred. Christian writers have therefore in most cases limited their discussion of the Incarnation to the context of man's fallen state. But there are a few who have ventured to take a wider view, most notably St Isaac the Syrian and St Maximus the Confessor in the East, and Duns Scotus in the West. The Incarnation, says St Isaac, is the most blessed and joyful thing that could possibly have happened to the human race. Can it be right, then, to assign as cause for this joyful happening something which might never have occurred, and indeed ought never to have done so? Surely, St Isaac urges, God's taking of our humanity is to be understood not only as an act of restoration, not only as a response to man's sin, but also and more fundamentally as an act of love, an expression of God's own nature. Even had there been no fall, God in his limitless, outgoing love would still have chosen to identify himself with his creation by becoming man.

The Incarnation of Christ, looked at in this way, effects more than a reversal of the fall, more than a restoration of man to his original state in Paradise. When God becomes man, this marks the beginning of an essentially new stage in the history of man, and not just a return to the past. The Incarnation raises man to a new level; the last state is higher than the first. Only in Jesus Christ do we see revealed the full possibilities of our human nature; until he is born, the true implications of our personhood are still hidden from us. Christ's birth, as St Basil puts it, is 'the birthday of the whole human race'; Christ is the first perfect man — perfect, that is to say, not just in a potential sense, as Adam was in his innocence before the fall, but in the sense of the completely realized 'likeness'. The Incarnation, then, is not simply a way of undoing the effects of original sin, but it is an essential stage upon man's journey from the divine image to the divine likeness. The true image and likeness of God is Christ himself; and so, from the very first moment of man's creation in the image, the Incarnation of Christ was in some way already implied. The true reason for the Incarnation, then, lies not in man's sinfulness but in his unfallen nature as a being made in the divine image and capable of union with God.

Twofold yet One

The Orthodox faith in the Incarnation is summed up in the refrain to the Christmas hymn by St Romanos the Melodist: 'A new-born child, God before the ages'. Contained in this short phrase are three assertions:

1. Jesus Christ is fully and completely God.
2. Jesus Christ is fully and completely man.
3. Jesus Christ is not two persons but one.

This is spelt out in great detail by the Ecumenical Councils. Just as the first two among the seven were concerned with the doctrine of the Trinity (see p. 36), so the last five were concerned with that of the Incarnation.

The third Council (Ephesus, 431) stated that the Virgin Mary is *Theotokos,* 'Godbearer' or 'Mother of God'. Implicit in this title is an affirmation, not primarily about the Virgin, but about Christ: *God was born.* The Virgin is Mother, not of a human person united to the divine person of the Logos, but of a single, undivided person who is God and man at once.

The fourth Council (Chalcedon, 451) proclaimed that there are in Jesus Christ *two natures,* the one divine and the other human. According to his divine nature Christ is 'one in essence' (*homoousios*) with God the Father; according to his human nature he is *homoousios* with us men. According to his divine nature, that is to say, he is fully and completely God: he is the second person of the Trinity, the unique 'only-begotten' and eternal Son of the eternal Father, born from the Father before all ages. According to his human nature he is fully and completely man: born in Bethlehem as a human child from the Virgin Mary, he has not only a human body like ours, but a human soul and intellect. Yet, though the incarnate Christ exists 'in two natures', he is *one person,* single and undivided, and not two persons coexisting in the same body.

The fifth Council (Constantinople, 553), developing what was said by the third, taught that 'One of the Trinity suffered in the flesh'. Just as it is legitimate to say that God was born, so we are entitled to assert that *God died.* In each case, of course, we specify that it is God-made-man of whom this is said. God in his transcendence is subject neither to birth nor to death, but these things are indeed undergone by the Logos incarnate.

The sixth Council (Constantinople, 680-1), taking up what was said by the fourth, affirmed that, just as there are in Christ two natures, divine and human, so there are in Christ *not only a divine will but also a human will;* for if Christ did not have a human will like ours, he would not be truly a man as we are. Yet these two wills are not contrary and opposed to each other, for the human will is at all times freely obedient to the divine.

The seventh Council (Nicaea, 787), setting the seal on the four that went before, proclaimed that, since Christ became true man, it is legitimate to *depict his face* upon the holy ikons; and, since Christ is one person and not two, these ikons do not just show us his humanity in separation from his divinity, but they show us the one person of the eternal Logos incarnate.

There is thus a contrast in technical formulation between the doctrine of the Trinity and that of the Incarnation. In the case of the Trinity, we affirm one single, specific essence or nature in three persons; and by virtue of this specific unity of essence the three persons have only a single will or energy. In the case of the incarnate Christ, on the other hand, there are two natures, the one divine and the other human, but there is only a single person, the eternal Logos who has become man. And whereas the three divine persons of the Trinity have only a single will and energy, the one person of the Incarnate Christ has two wills and energies, depending respectively upon his two natures. Yet, although there are in the incarnate Christ two natures and two wills, this does not destroy the unity of his person: everything in the Gospels that is spoken, performed or suffered by Christ is to be ascribed to one and the same personal subject, the eternal Son of God who has now been born as man within space and time.

Underlying the conciliar definitions about Christ as God and man, there are two basic principles concerning our salvation. First, *only God can save us*. A prophet or teacher of righteousness cannot be the redeemer of the world. If, then, Christ is to be our Saviour, he must be fully and completely God. Secondly, *salvation must reach the point of human need*. Only if Christ is fully and completely a man as we are, can we men share in what he has done for us.

It would therefore be fatal to the doctrine of our salvation if we were to regard Christ in the way that the Arians did, as a kind of demi-God situated in a shadowy intermediate region between humanity and divinity. The Christian doctrine of our salvation demands that we shall be maximalists. We are not to think of him as 'half-in-half'. Jesus Christ is not fifty per cent God and fifty per cent man, but one hundred per cent God and one hundred per cent man. In the epigrammatic phrase of St Leo the

Great, he is *totus in suis, totus in nostris,* 'complete in what is his own, complete in what is ours'.

Complete in what is his own: Jesus Christ is our window into the divine realm, showing us what God is. 'No one has ever seen God; the only-begotten Son, who is in the bosom of the Father, has made him known to us' (John 1:18).

Complete in what is ours: Jesus Christ is the second Adam, showing us the true character of our own human personhood. God alone is the perfect man.

Who is God? Who am I? To both these questions Jesus Christ gives us the answer.

Salvation as Sharing

The Christian message of salvation can best be summed up in terms of *sharing,* of solidarity and identification. The notion of sharing is a key alike to the doctrine of God in Trinity and to the doctrine of God made man. The doctrine of the Trinity affirms that, just as man is authentically personal only when he shares with others, so God is not a single person dwelling alone, but three persons who share each other's life in perfect love. The Incarnation equally is a doctrine of sharing or participation. Christ shares to the full in what we are, and so he makes it possible for us to share in what he is, in his divine life and glory. He became what we are, so as to make us what he is.

St Paul expresses this metaphorically in terms of wealth and poverty: 'You know the grace of our Lord Jesus Christ: he was rich, yet for your sake he became poor, so that through his poverty you might become rich' (2 Cor. 8:9). Christ's riches are his eternal glory; Christ's poverty is his complete self-identification with our fallen human condition. In the words of an Orthodox Christmas hymn, 'Sharing wholly in our poverty, thou hast made divine our earthly nature through thy union with it and participation in it.' Christ shares in our death, and we share in his life; he 'empties himself' and we are 'exalted' (Phil. 2:5-9). God's descent makes possible man's ascent. St Maximus the Confessor writes: 'Ineffably the infinite limits itself, while the finite is expanded to the measure of the infinite.'

As Christ said at the Last Supper: 'The glory which thou hast given to me I have given to them, that they may be one, as we are one: I in them and thou in me, may they be perfectly united into one' (John 17:22-23). Christ enables us to share in the Father's divine glory. He is the bond and meeting-point: because he is man, he is one with us; because he is God, he is one with the Father. So through and in him we are one with God, and the Father's glory becomes our glory. God's Incarnation opens the way to man's deification. To be deified is, more specifically, to be 'christified': the divine likeness that we are called to attain is the likeness of Christ. It is through Jesus the God-man that we men are 'ingodded', 'divinized', made 'sharers in the divine nature' (2 Pet. 1:4). By assuming our humanity, Christ who is Son of God by nature has made us sons of God by grace. In him we are 'adopted' by God the Father, becoming sons-in-the-Son.

This notion of salvation as sharing implies two things in particular about the Incarnation. First, it implies that Christ took not only a human body like ours, but also a human spirit, mind and soul like ours. Sin, as we saw (p. 75), has its source not from below but from above; it is not physical in its origin, but spiritual. The aspect of man, then, that requires to be redeemed is not primarily his body but his will and his centre of moral choice. If Christ did not have a human mind, then this would fatally undermine the second principle of salvation, that divine salvation must reach the point of human need.

The importance of this principle was re-emphasized during the second half of the fourth century, when Apollinarius advanced the theory — for which he was quickly condemned as a heretic — that at the Incarnation Christ took only a human body, but no human intellect or rational soul. To this St Gregory the Theologian replied, 'The unassumed is unhealed'. Christ, that is to say, saves us by becoming what we are; he heals us by taking our broken humanity into himself, by 'assuming' it as his own, by entering into our human experience and by knowing it *from the inside*, as being himself one of us. But had his sharing of our humanity been in some way incomplete, then man's salvation would be likewise incomplete. If we believe that Christ has brought us a total salvation, then it follows that he has assumed *everything*.

Secondly, this notion of salvation as sharing implies — although many have been reluctant to say this openly — that Christ assumed not just unfallen but *fallen* human nature. As the Epistle to the Hebrews insists (and in all the New Testament there is no Christological text more important than this): 'We do not have a high priest who cannot be touched with the feeling of our infirmities; but he was in all points tempted exactly as we are, yet without sinning' (4:15). Christ lives out his life on earth under the conditions of the fall. He is not himself a sinful person, but in his solidarity with fallen man he accepts to the full the consequences of Adam's sin. He accepts to the full not only the physical consequences, such as weariness, bodily pain, and eventually the separation of body and soul in death. He accepts also the moral consequences, the loneliness, the alienation, the inward conflict. It may seem a bold thing to ascribe all this to the living God, but a consistent doctrine of the Incarnation requires nothing less. If Christ had merely assumed *un*fallen human nature, living out his earthly life in the situation of Adam in Paradise, then he would not have been touched with the feeling of *our* infirmities, nor would he have been tempted in everything exactly as *we* are. And in that case he would not be *our* Saviour.

St Paul goes so far as to write, 'God has made him who knew no sin to be sin for our sake' (2 Cor. 5:21). We are not to think here solely in terms of some juridical transaction, whereby Christ, himself guiltless, somehow has our guilt 'imputed' to him in an exterior manner. Much more is involved than this. Christ saves us by experiencing *from within,* as one of us, all that we suffer inwardly through living in a sinful world.

Why a Virgin Birth?

In the New Testament it is clearly stated that Jesus Christ's Mother was a virgin (Matt. 1:18, 23, 25). Our Lord has an eternal Father in heaven, but no father on earth. He was begotten outside time from the Father without a mother, and he was begotten within time from his Mother without a father. This belief in the Virgin Birth does not, however, in any way detract from the fullness of Christ's humanity. Although the Mother was a virgin, yet there was a real human birth of a genuinely human baby.

Yet why, we ask, should his birth as man have taken this special form? To this it may be answered that the Mother's virginity serves as a 'sign' of the Son's uniqueness. This it does in three closely connected ways. First, the fact that Christ has no earthly father means that he points always beyond his situation in space and time to his heavenly and eternal origin. Mary's child is *truly* man, but he is not *only* man; he is within history but also above history. His birth from a virgin emphasizes that, while immanent, he is also transcendent; although completely man, he is also perfect God.

Secondly, the fact that Christ's Mother was a virgin indicates that his birth is to be ascribed in a unique manner *to the divine initiative*. Although he is fully human, his birth was not the result of sexual union between man and woman, but it was in a special way the *direct* work of God.

Thirdly, Christ's birth from a virgin underlines that the Incarnation did not involve the coming into being of a new person. When a child is born from two human parents in the usual fashion, a new person begins to exist. But the person of the incarnate Christ is none other than the second person of the Holy Trinity. At Christ's birth, therefore, no new person came into existence, but the pre-existent person of the Son of God now began to live according to a human as well as a divine mode of being. So the Virgin Birth reflects Christ's eternal pre-existence.

Because the person of the incarnate Christ is the same as the person of the Logos, the Virgin Mary may rightly be given the title *Theotokos,* 'God-bearer'. She is mother, not of a human son joined to the divine Son, but of a human son who *is* the only-begotten Son of God. The son of Mary is the same person as the divine Son of God; and so, by virtue of the Incarnation, Mary is in very truth 'Mother of God'.

Orthodoxy, while holding in high honour the role of the Blessed Virgin as Christ's Mother, sees no need for any dogma of the 'Immaculate Conception'. As defined by the Roman Catholic Church in 1854, this doctrine states that Mary, from 'the first moment of her conception' by her mother St Anne, was exempted from 'all stain of original guilt'. Two points need to be kept in mind here. First, as already noted (pp. 80–81), Orthodoxy does not envisage the fall in Augustinian terms, as a taint of inherited guilt. If we Orthodox had accepted the Latin view of original guilt, then we might also have felt the need to affirm a doctrine of the Immaculate Conception. As it is, our terms of reference are different; the Latin dogma seems to us not so much erroneous as superfluous. Secondly, for Orthodoxy the Virgin Mary constitutes, together with St John the Baptist, the crown and culmination of Old Testament sanctity. She is a 'link' figure: the last and greatest of the righteous men and women of the Old Covenant, she is at the same time the hidden heart of the Apostolic Church (see Acts 1:14). But the doctrine of the Immaculate Conception seems to us to take the Virgin Mary out of the Old Covenant and to place her, by anticipation, entirely in the New. On the Latin teaching she no longer stands on the same footing as the other saints of the Old Testament, and so her role as 'link' is impaired.

Although not accepting the Latin doctrine of the Immaculate Conception, Orthodoxy in its liturgical worship addresses the Mother of God as 'spotless' (*achrantos*), 'all-holy' (*panagia*), 'altogether without stain' (*panamomos*). We Orthodox believe that after her death she was assumed into heaven, where she now dwells — with her body as well as her soul — in eternal glory with her Son. She is for us 'the joy of all creation' (The Liturgy of St Basil), 'flower of the human race and gate of heaven' (*Dogmatikon* in Tone One), 'precious treasure of the whole world' (St Cyril of Alexandria). And with St Ephrem the Syrian we say:

Thou alone, O Jesus, with thy Mother art beautiful in every way:
For there is no blemish in thee, my Lord, and no stain in thy Mother.

From this it can be seen how high a place of honour we Orthodox ascribe to the Holy Virgin in our theology and prayer. She is for us the supreme offering made by the human race to God. In the words of a Christmas hymn:

What shall we offer thee, O Christ,
Who for our sakes hast appeared on earth as man?
Every creature made by thee offers thee thanks.
The angels offer thee a hymn; the heavens, a star;
The magi, gifts; the shepherds, their wonder;
The earth, its cave; the wilderness, a manger;
And we offer thee — a Virgin Mother.

Obedient unto Death

Christ's Incarnation is already an act of salvation. By taking up our broken humanity into himself, Christ restores it and, in the words of another Christmas hymn, 'lifts up the fallen image'. But in that case why was a death on the Cross necessary? Was it not enough for one of the Trinity to *live* as a man on earth, to think, feel and will as a man, without also having to *die* as a man?

In an unfallen world the Incarnation of Christ would indeed have sufficed as the perfect expression of God's outgoing love. But in a fallen and sinful world his love had to reach out yet further. Because of the tragic presence of sin and evil, the work of man's restoration was to prove infinitely costly. A *sacrificial* act of healing was required, a sacrifice such as only a suffering and crucified God could offer.

The Incarnation, it was said, is an act of identification and sharing. God saves us by identifying himself with us, by knowing our human experience from the inside. The Cross signifies, in the most stark and uncompromising manner, that this act of sharing is carried to the utmost limits. God incarnate enters into *all* our experience. Jesus Christ our companion shares not only in the fullness of human life but also in the fullness of human death. 'Surely he has borne our griefs and carried our sorrows' (Isa. 53:4) — *all* our griefs, *all* our sorrows. 'The unassumed is unhealed': but Christ our healer has assumed into himself everything, even death.

Death has both a physical and a spiritual aspect, and of the two it is the spiritual that is the more terrible. Physical death is the separation of man's body from his soul; spiritual death, the separation of man's soul from God. When we say that Christ became 'obedient unto death' (Phil. 2:8), we are not to limit these words to physical death alone. We should not think only of the bodily sufferings which Christ endured at his Passion — the scourging, the stumbling beneath the weight of the Cross, the nails, the thirst and heat, the torment of hanging stretched on the wood. The true meaning of the Passion is to be found, not in this only, but much more in his spiritual sufferings — in his sense of failure, isolation and utter loneliness, in the pain of love offered but rejected.

The Gospels are understandably reticent in speaking about this inward suffering, yet they provide us with certain glimpses. First, there is Christ's Agony in the garden of Gethsemane, when he is overwhelmed by horror and dismay, when he prays in anguish to his Father, 'If it is possible, let this cup pass from me' (Matt. 26:39), and when his sweat falls to the ground 'like great drops of blood' (Luke 22:44). Gethsemane, as Metropolitan Antony of Kiev insisted, provides the key to our whole doctrine of the Atonement. Christ is here confronted by a choice. Under no compulsion to die, freely he chooses to do so; and by this act of voluntary self-offering he turns what would have been a piece of arbitrary violence, a judicial murder, into a redemptive sacrifice. But this act of free choice is immensely difficult. Resolving to go forward to arrest and crucifixion, Jesus experiences, in the words of William Law, 'the anguishing terrors of a lost soul . . . the reality of eternal death'. Full weight must be given to Christ's words at Gethsemane, 'My soul is exceedingly sorrowful, even unto death' (Matt. 26:38). Jesus enters at this moment totally into the experience of spiritual death. He is at this moment identifying himself with all the despair and mental pain of humanity; and this identification is far more important to us than his participation in our physical pain.

A second glimpse is given us at the Crucifixion, when Christ cries out with a loud voice, 'My God, my God, why hast thou forsaken me?' (Matt. 27:46). Once again, full weight should be given to these words. Here is the extreme point of Christ's desolation, when he feels abandoned not only by men but by God. We cannot begin to explain how it is possible for one who is himself the living God to lose awareness of the divine presence. But this at least is evident. In Christ's Passion there is no play-acting, nothing is done for outward show. Each word from the Cross means what it says. And if the cry 'My God, my God. . .' is to signify anything at all, it must mean that at this moment Jesus is truly experiencing the spiritual death of separation from God. Not only does he shed his blood for us, but for our sakes he accepts even the loss of God.

'He descended into hell' (Apostles' Creed). Does this mean merely that Christ went to preach to the departed spirits during the interval between Great Friday evening and Easter morning (see 1 Pet. 3:19)? Surely it has also a deeper sense. Hell is a point not in space but in the soul. It is *the place where God is not.* (And yet God is everywhere!) If Christ truly 'descended into hell', that means he descended into the depths of the absence of God. Totally, unreservedly, he identified himself with all man's anguish and alienation. He assumed it into himself, and by assuming it he healed it. There was no other way he could heal it, except by making it his own.

Such is the message of the Cross to each one of us. However far I have to travel through the valley of the shadow of death, *I am never alone.* I have a companion. And this companion is not only a true man as I am, but also true God from true God. At the moment of Christ's deepest humiliation on the Cross, he is as much the eternal and living God as he is at his Transfiguration in glory upon Mount Tabor. Looking upon Christ crucified, I see not only a suffering man but *suffering God.*

Death as Victory

Christ's death upon the Cross is not a failure which was somehow put right afterwards by his Resurrection. In itself the death upon the Cross is a victory. The victory of what? There can be only one answer: *The victory of suffering love.* 'Love is strong as death. . . Many waters· cannot quench love' (Song of Songs 8:6-7). The Cross shows us a love that is strong as death, a love that is even stronger.

St John introduces his account of the Last Supper and the Passion with these words: 'Having loved his own which were in the world, he loved them to the end' (13:1). 'To the end' — the Greek says *eis telos,* meaning 'to the last', 'to the uttermost'. And this word *telos* is taken up later in the final cry uttered by Christ on the Cross: 'It is finished', *tetelestai* (John 19:30). This is to be understood, not as a cry of resignation or despair, but as a cry of victory: It is completed, it is accomplished, it is fulfilled.

What has been fulfilled? We reply: The work of suffering love, the victory of love over hatred. Christ our God has loved his own to the uttermost. Because of love he created the world, because of love he was born into this world as a man, because of love he took up our broken humanity into himself and made it his own. Because of love he identified himself with all our distress. Because of love he offered himself as a sacrifice, choosing at Gethsemane to go voluntarily to his Passion: 'I lay down my life for my sheep. . . No one takes it from me, but I lay it down of myself' (John 10:15, 18). It was willing love, not exterior compulsion, that brought Jesus to his death. At his Agony in the garden and at his Crucifixion the forces of darkness assail him with all their violence, but they cannot change his compassion into hatred; they cannot prevent his love from continuing to be itself. His love is tested to the furthest point, but it is not overwhelmed. 'The light shines on in the darkness, and the darkness has not swallowed it up' (John 1:5). To Christ's victory upon the Cross we may apply the words spoken by a Russian priest on his release from prison camp: 'Suffering has destroyed all things. One thing alone has stood firm — it is love.'

The Cross, understood as victory, sets before us the paradox of love's omnipotence. Dostoevsky comes near to the true meaning of Christ's victory in some statements which he puts into the mouth of *Starets* Zosima:

At some thoughts a man stands perplexed, above all at the sight of human sin, and he wonders whether to combat it by force or by humble love. Always decide: 'I will combat it by humble love.' If you resolve on that once for all, you can conquer the whole world. Loving humility is a terrible force: it is the strongest of all things, and there is nothing else like it.

Loving humility is a terrible force: whenever we give up anything or suffer anything, not with a sense of rebellious bitterness, but willingly and out of love, this makes us not weaker but stronger. So it is, above all, in the case of Jesus Christ. 'His weakness was of strength', says St Augustine. The power of God is shown, not so much in his creation of the world or in any of his miracles, but rather in the fact that out of love God has 'emptied himself' (Phil. 2:7), has poured himself out in generous self-giving, by his own free choice consenting to suffer and to die. And this self-emptying is a self-fulfilment:

kenosis is *plerosis*. God is never so strong as when he is most weak.

Love and hatred are not merely subjective feelings, affecting the inward universe of those who experience them, but they are also objective forces, altering the world outside ourselves. By loving or hating another, I cause the other in some measure to become that which I see in him or her. Not for myself alone, but for the lives of all around me, my love is creative, just as my hatred is destructive. And if this is true of my love, it is true to an incomparably greater extent of Christ's love. The victory of his suffering love upon the Cross does not merely set me an example, showing me what I myself may achieve if by my own efforts I imitate him. Much more than this, his suffering love has a creative effect upon me, transforming my own heart and will, releasing me from bondage, making me whole, rendering it possible for me to love in a way that would lie altogether beyond my powers, had I not first been loved by him. Because in love he has identified himself with me, his victory is my victory. And so Christ's death upon the Cross is truly, as the Liturgy of St Basil describes it, a 'life-creating death'.

Christ's suffering and death have, then, an objective value: he has done for us something we should be altogether incapable of doing without him. At the same time, we should not say that Christ has suffered 'instead of us', but rather that he has suffered *on our behalf*. The Son of God suffered 'unto death', not that we might be exempt from suffering, but that our suffering might be like his. Christ offers us, not a way *round* suffering, but a way *through* it; not substitution, but saving companionship.

Such is the value of Christ's Cross for us. Taken

closely in conjunction with the Incarnation and the Transfiguration which precede it, and with the Resurrection which follows it — for all these are inseparable parts of a single action or 'drama' — the Crucifixion is to be understood as the supreme and perfect *victory, sacrifice* and *example*. And in each case the victory, sacrifice and example is that of *suffering love*. So we see in the Cross:

the perfect victory of loving humility over hatred and fear;

the perfect sacrifice or voluntary self-offering of loving compassion;

the perfect example of love's creative power.

In the words of Julian of Norwich:

Wouldst thou learn thy Lord's meaning in this thing? Learn it well: Love was his meaning. Who showed it thee? Love. What showed he thee? Love. Wherefore showed it he? For Love. Hold thou therein and thou shalt learn and know more in the same. But thou shalt never know nor learn therein other thing without end. . . Then said our good Lord Jesus Christ: Art thou well pleased that I suffered for thee? *I said:* Yea, good Lord, I thank thee; Yea, good Lord, blessed mayst thou be. *Then said Jesus, our kind Lord:* If thou art pleased, I am pleased: it is a joy, a bliss, an endless satisfying to me that ever I suffered Passion for thee; and if I might suffer more, I would suffer more.

Christ is risen

Because Christ our God is true man, he died a full and genuine human death upon the Cross. But because he is not only true man but true God, because he is life itself and the source of life, this death was not and could not be the final conclusion.

The Crucifixion is itself a victory; but on Great Friday the victory is hidden, whereas on Easter morning it is made manifest. Christ rises from the dead, and by his rising he delivers us from anxiety and terror: the victory of the Cross is confirmed, love is openly shown to be stronger than hatred, and life to be stronger than death. God himself has died and risen from the dead, and so there is no more death: even death is filled with God. Because Christ is risen, we need no longer be afraid of any dark or evil force in the universe. As we proclaim each year at the Paschal midnight service, in words attributed to St John Chrysostom:

Let none fear death, for the death of the Saviour has set us free.
Christ is risen and the demons have fallen.
Christ is risen and the angels rejoice.

Here, as elsewhere, Orthodoxy is maximalist. We repeat with St Paul, 'If Christ is not risen, then is our preaching vain, and your faith is also vain' (1 Cor. 15:14). How shall we continue to be Christians, if we believe Christianity to be founded on a delusion? Just as it is not adequate to treat Christ merely as a prophet or a teacher of righteousness, and not as God incarnate, so it is not sufficient to explain away the Resurrection by saying that Christ's 'spirit' somehow lived on among his disciples. One who is not 'true God from true God', who has not conquered death by dying and rising from the dead, cannot be our salvation and our hope. We Orthodox believe that there was a genuine resurrection from the dead, in the sense that Christ's human body was reunited to his human soul, and that the tomb was found to be empty. For us Orthodox, when we engage in 'ecumenical' dialogues, one of the most significant divisions among contemporary Christians is between those who believe in the Resurrection and those who do not.

'You are witnesses of these things' (Luke 24:48). The risen Christ sends us out into the world to share with others the 'great joy' of his Resurrection. Fr Alexander Schmemann writes:

From its very beginning Christianity has been the proclamation of joy, of the only possible joy on earth. . . Without the proclamation of this joy Christianity is incomprehensible. It is only as joy that the Church was victorious in the world and it lost the world when it lost the joy, when it ceased to be a witness of it. Of all accusations against Christians, the most terrible one was uttered by Nietzsche when he said that Christians had no joy. . . 'For behold, I bring you tidings of great joy' — thus begins the Gospel, and its end is: 'And they worshipped him and returned to Jerusalem with great joy. . .' (Luke 2:10;24:52). And we must recover the meaning of this great joy.

An old man used to say: 'Spread abroad the name of Jesus in humility and with a meek heart; show him your feebleness, and he will become your strength.'
The Sayings of the Desert Fathers

How easy it is to say with every breath: 'My Lord Jesus, have mercy upon me! I bless you, my Lord Jesus, help me!'
St Macarius of Egypt

Into the black, yawning grave fly all hopes, plans, habits, calculations, and — above all — meaning: the meaning of life. Meaning has lost its meaning, and another incomprehensible Meaning has caused wings to grow at one's back. . . And I think that anyone who has had this experience of eternity, if only once; who has understood the way he is going, if only once; who has seen the One who goes before him, if only once — such a person will find it hard to turn aside from this path: to him all comfort will seem ephemeral, all treasures valueless, all companions unnecessary, if amongst them he fails to see the One Companion, carrying his Cross.

Mother Maria of Paris
(lines written after the death of her child)

Truth for us is not a system of thought. Truth is not created. Truth is. *Christ* is *the truth. Truth is a* person. *Truth is not limited within our apprehension of it. Truth transcends us; we can never come to the full comprehension of Truth.*

The search for Truth is the search for the person of Christ.

Truth is the Mystery of the person of Christ; and, because it is a person, the Mystery is inseparably linked with the event: the event of the encounter. Mystery and event are one.

The Mystery, for the Orthodox mind, is a precise and austere reality. It is Christ, and it is to meet Christ.

Mother Maria of Normanby

The Lord has become everything for you, and you

must become everything for the Lord.

St John of Kronstadt

The whole man would not have been saved, unless he had taken upon himself the whole man.

Origen

A marvellous wonder has this day come to pass:
Nature is made new, and God becomes man.
That which he was, he has remained;
And that which he was not, he has taken on himself
While suffering neither confusion nor division.

How shall I tell of this great mystery?
He who is without flesh becomes incarnate;
The Word puts on a body;
The Invisible is seen;
He whom no hand can touch is handled;
And he who has no beginning now begins to be.
The Son of God becomes the Son of man:
Jesus Christ, the same yesterday, today and for ever.

From Vespers on Christmas Day

Whom have we, Lord, like you —
The Great One who became small, the Wakeful who slept,
The Pure One who was baptized, the Living One

who died,
The King who abased himself to ensure honour
 for all.
Blessed is your honour!

It is right that man should acknowledge your divi-
 nity,
It is right for heavenly beings to worship your
 humanity.
The heavenly beings were amazed to see how
 small you became,
And earthly ones to see how exalted.

St Ephrem the Syrian

Because Christ is perfect Love, his life on earth can
never become a life of the past. He remains present to
all eternity. Then he was alone, and bore the sins of
men as one whole, alone. But, in death, he took us
all into his work. Therefore the Gospel is now pres-
ent with us. We may enter inside his own sacrifice.

Mother Maria of Normanby

He whom none may touch is seized;
He who looses Adam from the curse is bound.
He who tries the hearts and inner thoughts of man
 is unjustly brought to trial;
He who closed the abyss is shut in prison.
He before whom the powers of heaven stand with
 trembling stands before Pilate;
The Creator is struck by the hand of his creature.
He who comes to judge the living and the dead is

condemned to the Cross;
The Destroyer of hell is enclosed in a tomb.
O thou who dost endure all these things in thy
*   tender love,*
Who hast saved all men from the curse,
O longsuffering Lord, glory to thee.

From Vespers on Great Friday

The deepest foundation of the hope and joy which characterize Orthodoxy and which penetrate all its worship is the Resurrection. Easter, the centre of Orthodox worship, is an explosion of joy, the same joy which the disciples felt when they saw the risen Saviour. It is the explosion of cosmic joy at the triumph of life, after the overwhelming sorrow over death — death which even the Lord of life had to suffer when he became man. 'Let the heavens rejoice and the earth exult, and let all the world invisible and visible keep holiday, for Christ our eternal joy is risen.' All things are now filled with the certainty of life, whereas before all had been moving steadily towards death.

Orthodoxy emphasizes with special insistence the faith of Christianity in the triumph of life.

Fr Dumitru Staniloae

It is only by being a prisoner for religious convictions in a Soviet camp that one can really understand the mystery of the fall of the first man, the mystical meaning of the redemption of all creation, and the great victory of Christ over the forces of evil. It is only when we suffer for the ideals of the Holy Gospel that we can realize our sinful infirmity and our unworthiness in comparison with the great martyrs of the first Christian Church. Only then can we grasp the absolute necessity for profound meekness and humility, without which we cannot be saved; only then can we begin to discern the passing image of the seen, and the eternal life of the Unseen.

On Easter Day all of us who were imprisoned for religious convictions were united in the one joy of Christ. We were all taken into one feeling, into one spiritual triumph, glorifying the one eternal God. There was no solemn Paschal service with the ringing of church bells, no possibility in our camp to gather for worship, to dress up for the festival, to prepare Easter dishes. On the contrary, there was even more work and more interference than usual. All the prisoners here for religious convictions, whatever their denomination, were surrounded by more spying, by more threats from the secret police.

Yet Easter was there: great, holy, spiritual, unforgettable. It was blessed by the presence of our risen God among us — blessed by the silent Siberian stars and by our sorrows. How our hearts beat joyfully in communion with the great Resurrection! Death is conquered, fear no more, an eternal Easter is given to us! Full of this marvellous Easter, we send you from our prison camp the victorious and joyful tidings: Christ is risen!

Letter from a Soviet concentration camp

CHAPTER 5

GOD AS SPIRIT

The Spirit of God which has been given to this our flesh cannot endure sadness or restraint.

The Shepherd of Hermas

When the Spirit of God descends upon a man and overshadows him with the fullness of his out-pouring, then his soul overflows with a joy not to be described, for the Holy Spirit turns to joy whatever he touches.

The kingdom of heaven is peace and joy in the Holy Spirit.

Acquire inward peace, and thousands around you will find their salvation.

St Seraphim of Sarov

Clenched fist or opened hands?

On the walls of the catacombs in Rome there is sometimes painted the figure of a woman praying, the *Orans.* She is gazing towards heaven, her open hands raised with the palms upwards. This is one of the most ancient of Christian ikons. Whom does she represent — the Blessed Virgin Mary, the Church, or the soul at prayer? Or perhaps all three at once? However it is interpreted, this ikon depicts a basic Christian attitude: that of invocation or *epiclesis,* of calling down or waiting upon the Holy Spirit.

There are three main positions that we can assume with our hands, and each has its own sym-bolic meaning. Our hands may be closed, our fists clenched, as a gesture of defiance or in an effort to grasp and to hold fast, thus expressing aggression or fear. At the other extreme our hands may hang listlessly by our sides, neither defiant nor receptive. Or else, as a third possibility, our hands may be lifted up like those of the *Orans,* no longer clenched but open, no longer listless but ready to receive the gifts of the Spirit. An all-important lesson upon the spiritual Way is understanding how to unclench our fists and to open our hands. Each hour and minute we are to make our own the action of the *Orans*: invisibly we are to lift our opened hands to heaven, saying to the Spirit, *Come.*

The whole aim of the Christian life is to be a Spirit-bearer, to live in the Spirit of God, to breathe the Spirit of God.

The Wind and the Fire

There is a secret and hidden quality about the Holy Spirit, which makes it hard to speak or write about him. As St Symeon the New Theologian puts it:

> *He derives his name from the matter on which he rests,*
> *For he has no distinctive name among men.*

Elsewhere St Symeon writes (not, it is true, with specific reference to the Spirit, but his words apply very well to the third person of the Trinity):

> *It is invisible, and no hand can lay hold of it;*
> *Intangible, and yet it can be felt everywhere. . .*
> *What is it? O wonder! What is it not? For it has no name.*
> *In my foolishness I tried to grasp it,*
> *And I closed my hand, thinking that I held it fast:*
> *But it escaped, and I could not retain it in my*

> *fingers.*
> *Full of sadness, I unclenched my grip*
> *And I saw it once again in the palm of my hand.*
> *O unutterable wonder! O strange mystery!*
> *Why do we trouble ourselves in vain? Why do we*
>   *all wander astray?*

This elusiveness is evident in the symbols used by Scripture to point towards the Spirit. He is like 'a rushing, mighty wind' (Acts 2:2): his very title 'Spirit' (in Greek, *pneuma*) signifies wind or breath. As Jesus says to Nicodemus: 'The wind (*or* spirit) blows where it wishes; you hear the sound of it, but you do not know where it comes from, or where it is going' (John 3:8). We know that the wind is there, we hear it in the trees as we lie awake at night, we feel it on our faces as we walk on the hills. But if we try to grasp and hold it in our hands, it is lost. So it is with the Spirit of God. We cannot weigh and measure the Spirit, or keep it in a box under lock and key. In one of his poems Gerard Manley Hopkins likens the Blessed Virgin Mary to the air we breathe: the same analogy may be applied equally to the Spirit. Like the air, the Spirit is source of life, 'everywhere present and filling all things', always around us, always within us. Just as the air remains itself invisible to us but acts as the medium through which we see and hear other things, so the Spirit does not reveal to us his own face, but shows us always the face of Christ.

In the Bible the Holy Spirit is also likened to fire. When the Paraclete comes down upon the first Christians on the day of Pentecost, it is in 'cloven tongues, as of fire' (Acts 2:3). Like the wind, fire is elusive: alive, free, ever moving, not to be measured, weighed, or constricted within narrow limits. We feel the heat of the flames, but we cannot enclose and retain them in our hands.

Such is our relationship to the Spirit. We are conscious of his presence, we know his power, but we cannot easily picture to ourselves his person. The second person of the Trinity became incarnate, living on earth as man; the Gospels tell us of his words and actions, his face looks at us from the holy ikons, and so it is not difficult to picture him in our hearts. But the Spirit did not become incarnate; his divine person is not revealed to us in human form. In the case of the second person of the Trinity, the term 'generation' or 'being born', employed to indicate his eternal origin from the Father, conveys to our minds a distinct idea, a specific concept, although we realize that this concept is not to be interpreted literally. But the term used to denote the Spirit's eternal relationship to the Father, 'procession' or 'proceeding', conveys no clear and distinct idea. It is like a sacred hieroglyph, pointing to a mystery not yet plainly disclosed. The term indicates that the relationship between the Spirit and the Father is not the same as that between the Son and the Father; but what the exact nature of the difference may be, we are not told. This is inevitable, for the action of the Holy Spirit cannot be defined verbally. It has to be lived and experienced directly.

Yet, despite this arcane quality in the Holy Spirit, the Orthodox tradition firmly teaches two things about him. First, the Spirit is a *person*. He is not just a 'divine blast' (as once I heard someone describe him), not just an insentient force, but one of the three eternal persons of the Trinity; and so, for all his seeming elusiveness, we can and do enter into a personal 'I-Thou' relationship with him. Secondly, the Spirit, as the third member of the

Holy Triad, is *coequal* and *coeternal* with the other two; he is not merely a function dependent upon them or an intermediary that they employ. One of the chief reasons why the Orthodox Church rejects the Latin addition of the *filioque* to the Creed (p. 40), as also the Western teaching about the 'double procession' of the Spirit which lies behind this addition, is precisely our fear that such teaching might lead men to *depersonalize* and *subordinate* the Holy Spirit.

The coeternity and coequality of the Spirit is a recurrent theme in the Orthodox hymns for the Feast of Pentecost:

The Holy Spirit for ever was, and is, and shall be;
He has neither beginning nor ending,
But he is always joined and numbered with the
*   Father and the Son:*
Life and Giver of Life,
Light and Bestower of Light,
Love itself and Source of Love:
Through him the Father is made known,
Through him the Son is glorified and revealed to
*   all.*
One is the power, one is the structure,
One is the worship of the Holy Trinity.

The Spirit and the Son

Between the Father's 'two hands', his Son and his Spirit, there exists a reciprocal relationship, a bond of mutual service. There is often a tendency to express the inter-relation between the two in a one-sided manner that obscures this reciprocity. Christ, it is said, comes first; then, after his Ascension into heaven, he sends down the Spirit at Pentecost. But in reality the mutual links are more complex and more balanced. Christ sends the Spirit to us, but at the same time it is the Spirit that sends Christ. Let us recall and develop some of the Trinitarian patterns outlined above (p. 44).

1. *Incarnation.* At the Annunciation the Holy Spirit descends upon the Virgin Mary, and she conceives the Logos: according to the Creed, Jesus Christ was 'incarnate from the Holy Spirit and the Virgin Mary'. Here it is the Spirit who is sending Christ into the world.

2. *Baptism.* The relationship is the same. As Jesus comes up from the waters of Jordan, the Spirit descends upon him in the form of a dove: so it is the Spirit that 'commissions' Christ and sends him out to his public ministry. This is made abundantly clear in the incidents which follow immediately after the Baptism. The Spirit drives Christ into the wilderness (Mark 1:12), to undergo a forty-day period of testing before he begins to preach. When Christ returns at the end of this struggle, it is 'in the power of the Spirit' (Luke 4:14). The very first words of his preaching allude directly to the fact that it is the Spirit who is sending him: he reads Isaiah 61:1, applying the text to himself, 'The Spirit of the Lord is upon me, because he has anointed me to preach the Gospel to the poor' (Luke 4:18). His title 'Christ' or 'Messiah' signifies precisely that he is the one anointed by the Holy Spirit.

3. *Transfiguration.* Once more the Spirit descends upon Christ, this time not in the form of a dove but as a cloud of light. Just as the Spirit previously sent Jesus into the wilderness and then out to his public preaching, so now the Spirit sends him to his 'exodus' or sacrificial death at Jerusalem (Luke 9:31).

4. *Pentecost.* The mutual relationship is here

reversed. Hitherto it has been the Spirit who sends out Christ: now it is the risen Christ who sends out the Spirit. Pentecost forms the aim and completion of the Incarnation: in the words of St Athanasius, 'The Logos took flesh, that we might receive the Spirit.'

5. *The Christian Life.* But the reciprocity of the 'two hands' does not end here. Just as the Spirit sends the Son at the Annunciation, the Baptism and the Transfiguration, and just as the Son in his turn sends the Spirit at Pentecost, so after Pentecost it is the Spirit's task to bear witness to Christ, rendering the risen Lord ever present among us. If the aim of the Incarnation is the sending of the Spirit at Pentecost, the aim of Pentecost is the continuation of Christ's Incarnation within the life of the Church. This is precisely what the spirit does at the *epiclesis* in the Eucharistic consecration (p. 46); and this consecratory *epiclesis* serves as a model and paradigm for what is happening throughout our whole life in Christ.

'Where two or three are gathered together in my name, there am I in the midst of them' (Matt. 18:20). How is Christ present in our midst? *Through the Holy Spirit.* 'Lo, I am with you always, even to the end of the world' (Matt. 28:20). How is Christ always with us? *Through the Holy Spirit.* Because of the Comforter's presence in our heart, we do not simply know Christ at fourth or fifth hand, as a distant figure from long ago, about whom we possess factual information through written records; but we know him directly, here and now, in the present, as our personal Saviour and our friend. With the Apostle Thomas we can affirm, '*My* Lord and *my* God' (John 20:28). We do not say merely, 'Christ was born' — once, very long ago; we say 'Christ is born' — now, at this moment, in my own heart. We do not say merely 'Christ died', but 'Christ died for me'. We do not say merely, 'Christ rose', but 'Christ is risen' — he lives *now*, for me and in me. This immediacy and personal directness in our relationship with Jesus is precisely the work of the Spirit.

The Holy Spirit, then, does not speak to us about himself, but he speaks to us about Christ. 'When the Spirit of truth is come,' says Jesus at the Last Supper, 'he will guide you into all the truth; for he will not speak about himself. . . He will take what is mine, and will show it to you' (John 16:13-14). Herein lies the reason for the anonymity or, more exactly, the *transparency* of the Holy Spirit: he points, not to himself, but to the risen Christ.

The Pentecostal Gift

About the gift of the Paraclete on the day of Pentecost, three things are particularly striking:

First, it is a *gift to all God's people*: 'They were *all* filled with the Holy Spirit' (Acts 2:4). The gift or *charisma* of the Spirit is not conferred only upon bishops and clergy but upon each of the baptized. All are Spirit-bearers, all are — in the proper sense of the word — 'charismatics'.

Secondly, it is a *gift of unity*: 'They were all *with one accord* in one place' (Acts 2:1). The Holy Spirit makes the many to be one Body in Christ. The Spirit's descent at Pentecost reverses the effect of the tower of Babel (Gen. 11:7). As we say in one of the hymns for the Feast of Pentecost:

When the Most High came down and confused the
*   tongues,*
He divided the nations;

But when he distributed tongues of fire,
He called all to unity.
Therefore with one voice we glorify the All-Holy
  Spirit.

The Spirit brings unity and mutual comprehension, enabling us to speak 'with one voice'. He transforms individuals into persons. Of the first Christian community at Jerusalem, in the period immediately following Pentecost, it is stated that they 'had all things in common' and were 'united in heart and soul' (Acts 2:44; 4:32); and this should be the mark of the Pentecostal community of the Church in every age.

Thirdly, the gift of the Spirit is a *gift of diversity*: the tongues of fire are 'cloven' or 'divided' (Acts 2:3), and they are distributed to each one directly. Not only does the Holy Spirit make us all one, but he makes us each different. At Pentecost the multiplicity of tongues was not abolished, but it ceased to be a cause of separation; each spoke as before in his own tongue, but by the power of the Spirit each could understand the others. For me to be a Spirit-bearer is to realize all the distinctive characteristics in my personality; it is to become truly free, truly myself in my uniqueness. Life in the Spirit possesses an inexhaustible variety; it is wrong-doing, not sanctity, that is boring and repetitive. As a friend of mine, a priest who spent many hours each day hearing confessions, used to remark wearily: 'What a pity there are no new sins!' But there are always new forms of holiness.

Fathers in the Spirit and Fools

In the Orthodox tradition the direct action of the Paraclete within the Christian community is strikingly apparent in two 'Spirit-bearing' figures: the *elder* or spiritual father, and the *fool in Christ*.

The elder or 'old man', known in Greek as *geron* and in Russian as *starets,* need not necessarily be old in years, but he is wise in his experience of divine truth, and blessed with the grace of 'fatherhood in the Spirit', with the *charisma* of guiding others on the Way. What he offers to his spiritual children is not primarily moral instructions or a rule of life, but a personal relationship. 'A *starets*', says Dostoevsky, 'is one who takes your soul, your will, into his soul and his will.' Fr Zachariah's disciples used to say about him, 'It was as though he bore our hearts in his hands.'

The *starets* is the man of inward peace, at whose side thousands can find salvation. The Holy Spirit has given to him, as the fruit of his prayer and self-denial, the gift of discernment or discrimination, enabling him to read the secrets of men's hearts; and so he answers, not only the questions that others put to him, but also the questions — often much more fundamental — which they have not even thought of asking. Combined with the gift of discernment he possesses the gift of spiritual healing — the power to restore men's souls, and sometimes also their bodies. This spiritual healing he supplies, not only through his words of counsel, but through his silence and his very presence. Important though his advice may be, far more important is his intercessory prayer. He makes his children whole by praying constantly for them, by identifying himself with them, by accepting their joys and sorrows as his own, by taking on his shoulders the burden of their guilt or anxiety. No one can be a *starets* if he does not pray insistently for others.

If the *starets* is a priest, usually his ministry of spiritual direction is closely linked with the sacrament of confession. But a *starets* in the full sense, as described by Dostoevsky or exemplified by Fr Zachariah, is more than just a priest-confessor. A *starets* in the full sense cannot be appointed such by any superior authority. What happens is simply that the Holy Spirit, speaking directly to the hearts of the Christian people, makes it plain that this or that person has been blessed by God with the grace to guide and heal others. The true *starets* is in this sense a prophetic figure, not an institutional official. While most commonly a priest-monk, he may also be a married parish priest, or else a lay monk not ordained to the priesthood, or even — but this is less frequent — a nun, or a lay man or woman living in the outside world. If the *starets* is not himself a priest, after listening to people's problems and offering counsel, he will frequently send them to a priest for sacramental confession and absolution.

The relation between child and spiritual father varies widely. Some visit a *starets* perhaps only once or twice in a lifetime, at a moment of special crisis, while others are in regular contact with their *starets*, seeing him monthly or even daily. No rules can be laid down in advance; the association grows of itself under the immediate guidance of the Spirit.

Always the relationship is personal. The *starets* does not apply abstract rules learnt from a book — as in the 'casuistry' of Counter-Reformation Catholicism — but he sees on each occasion *this* particular man or woman who is before him; and, illumined by the Spirit, he seeks to transmit the unique will of God specifically for this one person. Because the true *starets* understands and respects the distinctive character of each one, he does not suppress their inward freedom but reinforces it. He does not aim at eliciting a mechanical obedience, but leads his children to the point of spiritual maturity where they can decide for themselves. To each one he shows his or her true face, which before was largely hidden from that person; and his word is creative and life-giving, enabling the other to accomplish tasks which previously seemed impossible. But all this the *starets* can achieve only because he loves each one personally. Moreover, the relationship is mutual: the *starets* cannot help another unless the other seriously desires to change his way of life and opens his heart in loving trust to the *starets*. He who goes to see a *starets* in a spirit of critical curiosity is likely to return with empty hands, unimpressed.

Because the relationship is always personal, a particular *starets* cannot help everyone equally. He can help only those who are specifically sent to him by the Spirit. Likewise the disciple should not say, 'My *starets* is better than all the others.' He should say only: 'My *starets* is the best for me.'

In guiding others, the spiritual father waits upon the will and voice of the Holy Spirit. 'I give only what God tells me to give', said St Seraphim. 'I believe the first word that comes to me to be inspired by the Holy Spirit.' Obviously no one has the right to act in this manner unless, through ascetic effort and prayer, he has attained an exceptionally intense awareness of God's presence. For anyone who has not reached this level, such behaviour would be presumptuous and irresponsible.

Fr Zachariah speaks in the same terms as St Seraphim:

Sometimes a man does not know himself what he will say. The Lord himself speaks through his lips. One must pray like this: 'O Lord, may you live in me, may you speak through me, may you act through me.' When the Lord speaks through a man's lips, then all the words of that man are effective and all that is spoken by him is fulfilled. The man who is speaking is himself surprised at this . . . Only one must not rely on wisdom.

The relationship between spiritual father and child extends beyond death to the Last Judgement. Fr Zachariah reassured his followers: 'After death I shall be much more alive than I am now, so don't grieve when I die. . . On the day of judgement the elder will say: *Here am I and my children*.' St Seraphim asked for these remarkable words to be inscribed on his tombstone:

When I am dead, come to me at my grave, and the more often the better. Whatever is on your soul, whatever may have happened to you, come to me as when I was alive and, kneeling on the ground, cast all your bitterness upon my grave. Tell me everything and I shall listen to you, and all the bitterness will fly away from you. And as you spoke to me when I was alive, do so now. For I am living, and I shall be for ever.

By no means all Orthodox have a spiritual father of their own. What are we to do if we search for a guide and cannot find one? It is of course possible to learn from books: whether or not we have a *starets*, we look to the Bible for constant guidance (see below, p. 146). But the difficulty with books is to know precisely what is applicable to me personally, at this specific point on my journey. As well as books, and as well as spiritual fatherhood, there is

also spiritual brotherhood or sisterhood — the help
that is given to us, not by teachers in God, but by
our fellow disciples. We are not to neglect the
opportunities offered to us in this form. But those
who seriously commit themselves to the Way
should in addition make every effort to find a father
in the Holy Spirit. If they seek humbly they will
undoubtedly be given the guidance that they
require. Not that they will often find a *starets* such
as St Seraphim or Fr Zachariah. We should take
care lest, in our expectation of something out-
wardly more spectacular, we overlook the help
which God is actually offering us. Someone who in
others' eyes is unremarkable will perhaps turn out
to be the one spiritual father who is able to speak *to
me, personally,* the words of fire that above all else I
need to hear.

A second prophetic Spirit-bearer within the
Christian community is the fool in Christ, called by
the Greeks *salos* and by the Russians *iurodivyi.*
Usually it is hard to discover how far his 'folly' is
consciously and deliberately assumed, and how far
it is spontaneous and involuntary. Inspired by the
Spirit, the fool carries the act of *metanoia* or
'change of mind' to its farthest extent. More radically than anyone else, he stands the pyramid on its
head. He is a living witness to the truth that Christ's
kingdom is not of this world; he testifies to the
reality of the 'anti-world', to the possibility of the
impossible. He practises an absolute voluntary
poverty, identifying himself with the humiliated
Christ. As Iulia de Beausobre puts it, 'He is nobody's son, nobody's brother, nobody's father, and
has no home.' Forgoing family life, he is the
wanderer or pilgrim who feels equally at home
everywhere, yet settles down nowhere. Clothed in

rags even in the winter cold, sleeping in a shed or church porch, he renounces not only material pos- sessions but also what others regard as his sanity and mental balance. Yet thereby he becomes a channel for the higher wisdom of the Spirit.

Folly for Christ's sake, needless to say, is an extremely rare vocation; nor is it easy to distinguish the counterfeit from the genuine, the 'breakdown' from the 'breakthrough'. There is in the end only one test: 'By their fruits you shall know them' (Matt. 7:20). The false fool is futile and destructive, to himself and to others. The true fool in Christ, possessing purity of heart, has upon the community around him an effect that is life-enhancing. From a practical point of view, no useful purpose is served by anything that the fool does. And yet, through some startling action or enigmatic word, often deliberately provocative and shocking, he awakens men from complacency and pharisaism. Remaining himself detached, he unleashes reactions in others, making the subconscious mount to the surface, and so enabling it to be purged and sanctified. He combines audacity with humility. Because he has renounced everything, he is truly free. Like the fool Nicolas of Pskov, who put into the hands of Tsar Ivan the Terrible a piece of meat dripping with blood, he can rebuke the powerful of this world with a boldness that others lack. He is the living conscience of society.

Become what you are

Only a few Christians in each generation become elders, and still fewer become fools in Christ. But *all* the baptized without exception are Spirit-bearers. 'Do you not realize or understand your

own nobility?' ask *The Homilies of St Macarius*.
'. . . Each of you has been anointed with the
heavenly Chrism, and has become a Christ by
grace; each is king and prophet of the heavenly
mysteries.'

What happened to the first Christians on the day
of Pentecost happens also to each of us when,
immediately following our Baptism, we are in the
Orthodox practice anointed with Chrism or *myron*.
(This, the second sacrament of Christian initiation,
corresponds to Confirmation in the Western tradition.) The newly-baptized, whether infant or adult,
is marked by the priest on the forehead, eyes, nos-
trils, mouth, ears, breast, hands and feet, with the
words, 'The seal of the gift of the Holy Spirit'. This
is for each one a personal Pentecost: the Spirit, who
descended visibly upon the Apostles in tongues of
fire, descends upon every one of us invisibly, yet·
with no less reality and power. Each becomes an
'anointed one', a 'Christ' after the likeness of Jesus
the Messiah. Each is sealed with the *charismata* of
the Comforter. From the moment of our Baptism
and Chrismation the Holy Spirit, together with
Christ, comes to dwell in the innermost shrine of
our heart. Although we say to the Spirit 'Come', he
is already within us.

However careless and indifferent the baptized
may be in their subsequent life, this indwelling presence of the Spirit is never totally withdrawn. But
unless we co-operate with God's grace — unless,
through the exercise of our free will, we struggle to
perform the commandments — it is likely that the
Spirit's presence within us will remain hidden and
unconscious. As pilgrims on the Way, then, it is our
purpose to advance from the stage where the grace
of the Spirit is present and active within us in a

hidden way, to the point of *conscious awareness*, when we know the Spirit's power openly, directly, with the full perception of our heart. 'I am come to cast fire on the earth,' Christ said, 'and how I wish it were already kindled!' (Luke 12:49). The Pentecostal spark of the Spirit, existing in each one of us from Baptism, is to be kindled into a living flame. We are to become what we are.

'The fruit of the Spirit is love, joy, peace, long-suffering, gentleness...' (Gal. 5:22). The conscious awareness of the Spirit's action should be something that permeates the whole of our inward life. It is not necessary for everyone to undergo a striking 'conversion experience'. Still less is it necessary for everyone to 'speak with tongues'. Most contemporary Orthodox view with deep reserve that part of the 'Pentecostal Movement' which treats 'tongues' as the decisive and indispensable proof that someone is truly a Spirit-bearer. The gift of 'tongues' was, of course, frequent in the Apostolic age; but since the middle of the second century it has been far less common, although it has never entirely disappeared. In any event, St Paul insists that this is one of the less important of spiritual gifts (see 1 Cor. 14:5).

When it is genuinely spiritual, 'speaking with tongues' seems to represent an act of 'letting go' — the crucial moment in the breaking-down of our sinful self-trust, and its replacement by a willingness to allow God to act within us. In the Orthodox tradition this act of 'letting-go' more often takes the form of the *gift of tears*. 'Tears', says St Isaac the Syrian, 'mark the frontier between the bodily and the spiritual state, between the state of subjection to the passions and that of purity.' And in a memorable passage he writes:

The fruits of the inner man begin only with the shedding of tears. When you reach the place of tears, then know that your spirit has come out from the prison of this world and has set its foot upon the path which leads towards the New Age. Your spirit begins at this moment to breathe the wonderful air which is there, and it starts to shed tears. The moment for the birth of the spiritual child is now at hand, and the travail of childbirth becomes intense. Grace, the common mother of us all, makes haste to give birth mystically to the soul, God's image, bringing it forth into the light of the Age to come. And when the time for the birth has arrived, the intellect begins to sense something of the things of that other world — as a faint perfume, or as the breath of life which a new-born child receives into its bodily frame. But we are not accustomed to such an experience and, finding it hard to endure, our body is suddenly overcome by a weeping mingled with joy.

There are, however, many kinds of tears, and not all are a gift of the Spirit. Besides spiritual tears, there are tears of anger and frustration, tears shed in self-pity, sentimental and emotional tears. Discernment is needed; hence the importance of seeking the help of an experienced spiritual guide, a *starets*. Discernment is even more necessary in the case of 'tongues'. Often it is not the Spirit of God that is speaking through the tongues, but the all-too-human spirit of auto-suggestion and mass hysteria. There are even occasions when 'speaking with tongues' is a form of demonic possession. 'Beloved, trust not every spirit, but test the spirits to see whether they are from God' (1 John 4:1).

Orthodoxy, therefore, while insisting upon the need for a direct experience of the Holy Spirit, insists also upon the need for discrimination and sobriety. Our weeping, and likewise our participation in the other gifts of the Spirit, need to be purged of all fantasy and emotional excitement. Gifts that are genuinely spiritual are not to be rejected, but we should never pursue such gifts as an end in themselves. Our aim in the life of prayer is not to gain feelings or 'sensible' experiences of any particular kind, but simply and solely to conform our will to God's. 'I seek not what is yours but you', says St Paul to the Corinthians (2 Cor. 12:14); and we say the same to God. We seek not the gifts but the Giver.

An Invocation to the Holy Spirit

> *Come, true light.*
> *Come, life eternal.*
> *Come, hidden mystery.*
> *Come, treasure without name.*
> *Come, reality beyond all words.*
> *Come, person beyond all understanding.*
> *Come, rejoicing without end.*
> *Come, light that knows no evening.*
> *Come, unfailing expectation of the saved.*
> *Come, raising of the fallen.*
> *Come, resurrection of the dead.*
> *Come, all-powerful, for unceasingly you create, refashion and change all things by your will alone.*
> *Come, invisible whom none may touch and handle.*
> *Come, for you continue always unmoved, yet at every instant you are wholly in movement; you draw near to us who lie in hell, yet you remain higher than the heavens.*

Come, for your name fills our hearts with longing
and is ever on our lips; yet who you are and
what your nature is, we cannot say or know.
Come, Alone to the alone.
Come, for you are yourself the desire that is within
me.
Come, my breath and my life.
Come, the consolation of my humble soul.
Come, my joy, my glory, my endless delight.
St Symeon the New Theologian

The Holy Spirit is light and life,
A living fountain of knowledge,
Spirit of wisdom,
Spirit of understanding,
Loving, righteous, filled with knowledge and
power,
Cleansing our offences,
God and making us god,
Fire that comes forth from Fire,
Speaking, working, distributing gifts of grace.
By him were all the prophets, the apostles of God
and the martyrs crowned.
Strange were the tidings, strange was the vision at
Pentecost:
Fire came down, bestowing gifts of grace on each.
From Vespers on the Feast of Pentecost

Everyone who has been baptized in an orthodox
manner has received secretly the fullness of grace;
and if he then goes on to perform the command-
ments, he will become consciously aware of this
grace within him.

However far a man may advance in faith, however
great the blessings that he attains, he never discovers,
nor can he ever discover, anything more than what

he has already received secretly through Baptism. Christ, being perfect God, bestows upon the baptized the perfect grace of the Spirit. We for our part cannot possibly add to that grace, but it is revealed and manifests itself to us increasingly, in proportion to our fulfilment of the commandments. Whatever, then, we offer to him after our regeneration, was already within us and came originally from him.

St Mark the Monk

The divine persons do not assert themselves, but one bears witness to another. It is for this reason that St John of Damascus said that 'the Son is the image of the Father, and the Spirit the image of the Son'. It follows that the third person of the Trinity is the only one not having his image in another person. The Holy Spirit, as person, remains unmanifested, hidden, concealing himself in his very appearing. . .

The Holy Spirit is the sovereign unction upon the Christ and upon all the Christians called to reign with him in the Age to come. It is then that this divine person, now unknown, not having his image in another member of the Trinity, will manifest himself in deified persons: for the multitude of the saints will be his image.

Vladimir Lossky

The Holy Spirit supplies all things:
He causes prophecies to spring up,
He sanctifies priests,
To the unlettered he taught wisdom,
The fishermen he turned into theologians.
He holds together in unity the whole structure of
*   the Church.*
One in essence and one in throne with the Father
*   and the Son,*

O Paraclete, glory to thee!
From Vespers on the Feast of Pentecost

CHAPTER 6

GOD AS PRAYER

Not I, but Christ in me.

Galatians 2:20

*There is no life without prayer. Without prayer there
is only madness and horror.*

*The soul of Orthodoxy consists in the gift of
prayer.*

Vasilii Rozanov

*The brethren asked Abba Agathon: 'Amongst all
our different activities, father, which is the virtue that
requires the greatest effort?' He answered: 'Forgive
me, but I think there is no labour greater than
praying to God. For every time a man wants to pray,
his enemies the demons try to prevent him; for they
know that nothing obstructs them so much as prayer
to God. In everything else that a man undertakes, if
he perseveres, he will attain rest. But in order to pray
a man must struggle to his last breath.'*

The Sayings of the Desert Fathers

The Three Stages on the Way

Shortly after being ordained priest, I asked a
Greek bishop for advice on the preaching of sermons. His reply was specific and concise. 'Every
sermon', he said, 'should contain three points:
neither less nor more.'

It is customary likewise to divide the spiritual

Way into three stages. For St Dionysius the Areopagite these are *purification, illumination* and *union* — a scheme often adopted in the West. St Gregory of Nyssa, taking as his model the life of Moses (see p. 15), speaks of *light, cloud* and *darkness*. But in this chapter we shall follow the somewhat different threefold scheme devised by Origen, rendered more precise by Evagrius, and fully developed by St Maximus the Confessor. The first stage here is *praktiki* or the practice of the virtues; the second stage is *physiki* or the contemplation of nature; the third and final stage, our journey's end, is *theologia* or 'theology' in the strict sense of the word, that is, the contemplation of God himself.

The first stage, the practice of the virtues, begins with repentance. The baptized Christian, by listening to his conscience and by exerting the power of his free will, struggles with God's help to escape from enslavement to passionate impulses. By fulfilling the commandments, by growing in his awareness of right and wrong and by developing his sense of 'ought', gradually he attains purity of heart; and it is this that constitutes the ultimate aim of the first stage. At the second stage, the contemplation of nature, the Christian sharpens his perception of the 'isness' of created things, and so discovers the Creator present in everything. This leads him to the third stage, the direct vision of God, who is not only in everything but above and beyond everything. At this third stage, no longer does the Christian experience God solely through the intermediary of his conscience or of created things, but he meets the Creator face to face in an unmediated union of love. The full vision of the divine glory is reserved for the Age to come, yet even in this present life the saints enjoy the sure pledge and firstfruits of the coming harvest.

Often the first stage is termed the 'active life', while the second and the third are grouped together and jointly designated the 'contemplative life'. When these phrases are used by Orthodox writers, they normally refer to inward spiritual states, not to outward conditions. It is not only the social worker or the missionary who is following the 'active life'; the hermit or recluse is likewise doing so, inasmuch as he or she is still struggling to overcome the passions and to grow in virtue. And in the same way the 'contemplative life' is not restricted to the desert or the monastic enclosure: a miner, typist or housewife may also possess inward silence and prayer of the heart, and may therefore be in the true sense a 'contemplative'. In *The Sayings of the Desert Fathers* we find the following story about St Antony, the greatest of solitaries: 'It was revealed to Abba Antony in the desert: "In the city there is someone who is your equal, a doctor by profession. Whatever he has to spare he gives to those in need, and all day long he sings the Thrice-Holy Hymn with the angels." '

The image of three stages on a journey, while useful, should not be taken too literally. Prayer is a living relationship between persons, and personal relationships cannot be neatly classified. In particular it should be emphasized that the three stages are not strictly consecutive, the one coming to an end before the next begins. Direct glimpses of the divine glory are sometimes conferred by God on a person as an unexpected gift, before that person has even begun to repent and to commit himself to the struggle of the 'active life'. Conversely, however deeply a man may be initiated by God into the mysteries of contemplation, so long as he lives on earth he must continue to fight against temptations; up to the very end of his time on earth he is still learning to repent. 'A man should expect temptation until his last breath', insists St Antony of Egypt. Elsewhere in *The Sayings of the Desert Fathers* there is a description of the death of Abba Sisois, one of the holiest and best loved of the 'old men'. The brothers standing round his bed saw that his lips were moving. 'Who are you talking to, father?' they asked. 'See', he replied, 'the angels have come to take me, and I am asking them for more time — more time to repent.' His disciples said, 'You have no need to repent.' But the old man said, 'Truly, I am not sure whether I have even begun to repent.' So his life ends. In the eyes of his spiritual children he was already perfect; but in his own eyes he was still at the very beginning.

No one, then, can ever claim in this life to have passed beyond the first stage. The three stages are not so much successive as simultaneous. We are to think of the spiritual life in terms of three deepening levels, interdependent, coexisting with each other.

Three Presuppositions

Before speaking further about these stages or levels, it will be wise to consider three indispensable elements, presupposed at every point upon the spiritual Way.

First, it is presupposed that the traveller on the Way is a *member of the Church*. The journey is undertaken in fellowship with others, not in isolation. The Orthodox tradition is intensely conscious of the ecclesial character of all true Christianity. Let us take up and complete an earlier citation from Aleksei Khomiakov (see p. 81):

No one is saved alone. He who is saved is saved in the Church, as a member of her and in union with all her other members. If anyone believes, he is in the communion of faith; if he loves, he is in the communion of love; if he prays, he is in the communion of prayer.

As Fr Alexander Elchaninov observes:

Ignorance and sin are characteristic of isolated individuals. Only in the unity of the Church do we find these defects overcome. Man finds his true self in the Church alone: not in the helplessness of spiritual isolation but in the strength of his communion with his brothers and his Saviour.

It is of course true that there are many who with their conscious brain reject Christ and his Church, or who have never heard of him; and yet, unknown to themselves, these people are true servants of the one Lord in their deep heart and in the implicit direction of their whole life. God is able to save those who in this life never belonged to his Church. But, looking at the matter from *our* side, this does not entitle any of us to say, 'The Church is unnecessary for me.' There is in Christianity no such thing as a spiritual *élite* exempt from the obligations of normal church membership. The solitary in the desert is as much a churchman as the artisan in the city. The ascetic and mystical path, while it is from one point of view 'the flight of the alone to the Alone', is yet at the same time essentially social and communal. The Christian is the one who has brothers and sisters. He belongs to a family — the family of the Church.

Secondly, the spiritual Way presupposes not only life in the Church but *life in the sacraments*. As Nicolas Cabasilas affirms with great emphasis, it is the sacraments that constitute our life in Christ. Here again there is no place for elitism. We are not to imagine that there is one path for the 'ordinary' Christian — the path of corporate worship, centred around the sacraments — and another path for a select few who are called to inner prayer. On the contrary there is only *one* way; the way of the sacraments and the way of inner prayer are not alternatives, but form a single unity. None can be truly a Christian without sharing in the sacraments, just as none can be truly a Christian if he treats the sacraments merely as a mechanical ritual. The hermit in the desert may receive communion less frequently than the Christian in the city; that does not mean, however, that the sacraments are any the less important to the hermit, but simply that the rhythm of his sacramental life is different. Certainly God is able to save those who have never been baptized. But while God is not bound to the sacraments, we are bound to them.

Earlier we noted, with St Mark the Monk (pp. 137-8), how the whole of the ascetic and mystical life is already contained in the sacrament of Baptism: however far a person advances upon the Way, all that he discovers is nothing else than the revelation or making manifest of baptismal grace. The same can be said of Holy Communion: the whole of the ascetic and mystical life is a deepening and realization of our Eucharistic union with Christ the Saviour. In the Orthodox Church communion is given to infants from the moment of their Baptism onwards. This means that the earliest childhood memories of the Church that an Orthodox Christian has will probably be linked with coming up to receive Christ's Body and Blood; and the last conscious action of his life, so he hopes, will also be the reception of the Divine Gifts. So his experience of Holy Communion extends over the whole range of his conscious life. It is above all through Communion that the Christian is made one with and in Christ, 'christified', 'ingodded' or 'deified'; it is above all through Communion that he receives the firstfruits of eternity. 'Blessed is he that has eaten the Bread of love which is Jesus', writes St Isaac the Syrian. 'While still in this world, he breathes the air of the resurrection, in which the righteous will delight after they rise from the dead.' 'All human striving reaches here its ultimate goal', says Nicolas Cabasilas. 'For in this sacrament we attain God himself, and God himself is made one with us in the most perfect of all possible unions. . . This is the final mystery: beyond this it is not possible to go, nor can anything be added to it.'

The spiritual Way is not only ecclesial and sacramental; it is also *evangelical*. This is the third indispensable presupposition for an Orthodox Christian. At each step upon the path, we turn for guidance to the voice of God speaking to us through the Bible. According to *The Sayings of the Desert Fathers*, 'The old men used to say: God demands nothing from Christians except that they shall hearken to the Holy Scriptures, and carry into effect the things that are said in them.' (But elsewhere *The Sayings* also insist on the importance of having the guidance of a spiritual father, to help us to apply Scripture aright.) When St Antony of Egypt was asked, 'What rules shall I keep so as to please God?', he replied: 'Wherever you go, have God always before your eyes; in whatever you do or say, have an example from the Holy Scriptures; and whatever the place in which you dwell, do not be quick to move elsewhere. Keep these three things, and you will live.' 'The only pure and all-sufficient source of the doctrines of the faith', writes Metropolitan Philaret of Moscow, 'is the revealed Word of God, contained in the Holy Scriptures.'

To one entering the monastery as a novice, Bishop Ignatii Brianchaninov gives these instructions, which certainly apply with equal force to lay people:

From his first entry into the monastery a monk should devote all possible care and attention to the reading of the Holy Gospel. He should study the Gospel so closely that it is always present in his memory. At every moral decison he takes, for every act, for every thought, he should always have ready in his memory the teaching of the Gospel. . . Keep on studying the Gospel until the end of your life. Never stop. Do not think that you know it enough, even if you know it all by heart.

What is the attitude of the Orthodox Church towards the critical study of the Bible, as it has been carried on in the West over the past two centuries? Since our reasoning brain is a gift from God, there is undoubtedly a legitimate place for scholarly research into Biblical origins. But, while we are not to reject this research wholesale, we cannot as Orthodox accept it in its entirety. Always we need to keep in view that the Bible is not just a collection of historical documents, but it is *the book of the Church, containing God's word.* And so we do not read the Bible as isolated individuals, interpreting it solely by the light of our private understanding, or in terms of current theories about source, form or redaction criticism. We read it as members of the Church, in communion with all the other members throughout the ages. The final criterion for our interpretation of Scripture is the *mind of the Church*. And this means keeping constantly in view how the meaning of Scripture is explained and applied in Holy Tradition: that is to say, how the Bible is understood by the Fathers and the saints, and how it is used in liturgical worship.

As we read the Bible, we are all the time gathering information, wrestling with the sense of obscure sentences, comparing and analysing. But this is secondary. The real purpose of Bible study is much more than this — to feed our love for Christ, to kindle our hearts into prayer, and to provide us with guidance in our personal life. The study of words should give place to an immediate dialogue with the living Word himself. 'Whenever you read the Gospel,' says St Tikhon of Zadonsk, 'Christ himself is speaking to you. And while you read, you are praying and talking with him.'

In this way Orthodox are encouraged to practise a slow and attentive reading of the Bible, in which our study leads us directly into prayer, as with the *lectio divina* of Benedictine and Cistercian monasticism. But usually Orthodox are not given detailed rules or methods for this attentive reading. The Orthodox spiritual tradition makes little use of systems of 'discursive meditation', such as were elaborated in the Counter-Reformation West by Ignatius Loyola or François de Sales. One reason why Orthodox have usually felt no need for such methods is that the liturgical services which they are attending, especially at Great Feasts and during Lent, are very lengthy and contain frequent repetitions of key texts and images. All this is sufficient to feed the spiritual imagination of the worshipper, so that he has no need in addition to rethink and develop the message of the church services in a daily period of formal meditation.

Approached in a prayerful manner, the Bible is found to be always contemporary — not just writings composed in the distant past but a message addressed directly to me here and now. 'He who is humble in his thoughts and engaged in spiritual work', says St Mark the Monk, 'when he reads the Holy Scriptures will apply everything to himself and not to someone else.' As a book uniquely inspired by God and addressed to each of the faithful personally, the Bible possesses sacramental power, transmitting grace to the reader, bringing him to a point of meeting and decisive encounter. Critical scholarship is by no means excluded, but the true meaning of the Bible will only be apparent to those who study it with their spiritual intellect as well as their reasoning brain.

Church, sacraments, Scripture — such are the presuppositions for our journey. Let us now consider the three stages: the active life or practice of the virtues, the contemplation of nature, the contemplation of God.

The Kingdom of Heaven suffers Violence

As its title implies, the active life requires on our side effort, struggle, the persistent exertion of our free will. 'Strait is the gate and narrow is the way that leads to life. . . Not everyone that says to me, Lord, Lord, shall enter into the kingdom of heaven, but he that does the will of my Father' (Matt. 7:14, 21). We are to hold in balance two complementary truths: without God's grace we *can* do nothing; but without our voluntary co-operation God *will* do nothing. 'The will of man is an essential condition, for without it God does nothing' (*The Homilies of St Macarius*). Our salvation results from the convergence of two factors, unequal in value yet both indispensable: divine initiative and human response. What God does is incomparably the more important, but man's participation is also required.

In an unfallen world man's response to divine love would be altogether spontaneous and joyful. Even in a fallen world the element of spontaneity and joy remains, but there is also the need to fight resolutely against the deeply-rooted habits and inclinations that are the result of sin, both original and personal. One of the most important qualities needed by the traveller on the Way is faithful perseverance. The endurance required from one who climbs a mountain physically is required likewise from those who would ascend the mountain of God.

Man must do violence to himself — to his fallen self, that is to say — for the kingdom of heaven suffers violence, and it is the men of violence who take it by force (Matt. 11:12). This we are told repeatedly by our guides upon the Way; and they are speaking, it should be remembered, to married Christians as well as to monks and nuns. 'God demands everything from a man — his mind, his reason, all his actions. . . Do you wish to be saved when you die? Go and exhaust yourself; go and labour; go, seek and you shall find; watch and knock, and it shall be opened to you' (*The Sayings of the Desert Fathers*). 'The present age is not a time for rest and sleep, but it is a struggle, a combat, a market, a school, a voyage. Therefore you must exert yourself, and not be downcast and idle, but devote yourself to holy actions' (*Starets* Nazarii of Valamo). 'Nothing comes without effort. The help of God is always ready and always near, but is given only to those who seek and work, and only to those seekers who, after putting all their powers to the test, then cry out with their whole heart: Lord, help us' (Bishop Theophan the Recluse). 'Where there is no sorrow there is no salvation' (St Seraphim of Sarov). 'To rest is the same as to retreat' (Tito Colliander). Yet, lest we should be too much downcast by this severity, we are also told: 'The whole of a man's life is but a single day, for those who labour with eagerness' (*The Sayings of the Desert Fathers*).

And what do all these words about exertion and suffering signify in practice? They mean that each day we are to renew our relationship with God through living prayer; and to pray, as Abba Agathon reminds us, is the hardest of all tasks. If we do not find prayer difficult, perhaps it is because we have not really started to pray. They mean also that each day we are to renew our relationship with others through imaginative sympathy, through acts of practical compassion, and through cutting off our own self-will. They mean that we are to take up the Cross of Christ, not once for all through a single grandiose gesture, but every day afresh: 'If any man will come after me, let him deny himself and take up his cross *daily*' (Luke 9:23). And yet this daily cross-bearing is at the same time a daily sharing in the Lord's Transfiguration and Resurrection: 'sorrowful, yet always rejoicing; poor, yet making many rich; having nothing, yet possessing all things. . . dying, and, behold, we live' (2 Cor. 6:9, 10).

A Change of Mind

Such is the general character of the active life. It is marked above all by four qualities: repentance, watchfulness, discrimination, and the guarding of the heart. Let us look briefly at each of these.

'The beginning of salvation is to condemn one-self' (Evagrius). *Repentance* marks the starting-point of our journey. The Greek term *metanoia,* as we have noted (p. 17), signifies primarily a 'change of mind'. Correctly understood, repentance is not negative but positive. It means, not self-pity or remorse, but conversion, the re-centering of our whole life upon the Trinity. It is to look, not back-ward with regret, but forward with hope — not downwards at our own shortcomings, but upwards at God's love. It is to see, not what we have failed to be, but what by divine grace we can now become; and it is to act upon what we see. To repent is to open our eyes to the light. In this sense, repentance is not just a single act, an initial step, but a contin-uing state, an attitude of heart and will that needs to be ceaselessly renewed up to the end of life. In the words of St Isaias of Sketis, 'God requires us to go on repenting until our last breath.' 'This life has been given you for repentance', says St Isaac the Syrian. 'Do not waste it on other things.'

To repent is to wake up. Repentance, change of mind, leads to *watchfulness*. The Greek term used here, *nepsis,* means literally sobriety and wakeful-ness — the opposite to a state of drugged or alco-holic stupor; and so in the context of the spiritual life it signifies attentiveness, vigilance, recollection. When the prodigal son repented, it is said that 'he came to himself' (Luke 15:17). The 'neptic' man is one who has come to himself, who does not day-dream, drifting aimlessly under the influence of passing impulses, but who possesses a sense of direction and purpose. As *The Gospel of Truth* (mid-second century) expresses it, 'He is like one who awakens from drunkenness, returning to him-self . . . He knows where he has come from and where he is going.'

Watchfulness means, among other things, to be *present where we are* — at this specific point in space, at this particular moment in time. All too often we are scattered and dispersed; we are living, not with alertness in the present, but with nostalgia in the past, or with misgiving and wishful thinking in the future. While we are indeed required responsibly to plan for the future — for watchfulness is the opposite of fecklessness — we are to think about the future only so far as it depends upon the present moment. Anxiety over remote possibilities which lie altogether beyond our immediate control is sheer waste of our spiritual energies.

The 'neptic' man, then, is gathered into the *here* and the *now*. He is the one who seizes the *kairos*, the decisive moment of opportunity. God, so C.S. Lewis remarks in *The Screwtape Letters*, wants men to attend chiefly to two things: 'to eternity itself, and to that point of time which they call the Present. For the Present is the point at which time touches eternity. Of the present moment, and of it only, humans have an experience which (God) has of reality as a whole; in it alone freedom and actuality are offered them.' As Meister Eckhart teaches, 'He who abides always in a present *now*, in him does God beget his Son without ceasing.'

The 'neptic' man is the one who understands this 'sacrament of the present moment', and who tries to live by it. He says to himself, in the words of Paul Evdokimov: 'The hour through which you are at present passing, the man whom you meet here and now, the task on which you are engaged at this very moment — these are always the most important in your whole life.' He makes his own the motto written on Ruskin's coat of arms: *Today, today,*

today. 'There is a voice which cries to a man until his last breath, and it says: Be converted today' (*The Sayings of the Desert Fathers*).

Growing in watchfulness and self-knowledge, the traveller upon the Way begins to acquire the power of *discrimination* or discernment (in Greek, *diakrisis*). This acts as a spiritual sense of taste. Just as the physical sense of taste, if healthy, tells a man at once whether food is mouldy or wholesome, so the spiritual taste, if developed through ascetic effort and prayer, enables a man to distinguish between the varying thoughts and impulses within him. He learns the difference between the evil and the good, between the superfluous and the meaningful, between the fantasies inspired by the devil and the images marked upon his creative imagination by celestial archetypes.

Through discrimination, then, a man begins to take more careful note of what is happening within him, and so he learns to *guard the heart,* shutting the door against the temptations or provocations of the enemy. 'Guard your heart with all diligence' (Prov. 4:23). When the heart is mentioned in Orthodox spiritual texts, it is to be understood in the full Biblical sense. The heart signifies not simply the physical organ in the chest, not simply the emotions and affections, but the spiritual centre of man's being, the human person as made in God's image — the deepest and truest self, the inner shrine to be entered only through sacrifice and death. The heart is thus closely related to the spiritual intellect, of which we have already spoken (p. 61); in some contexts the two terms are almost interchangeable. But 'heart' has often a more inclusive sense than 'intellect'. 'Prayer of the heart', in the Orthodox tradition, means prayer offered by the whole person, involving intellect, reason, will, affections, and also the physical body.

An essential aspect of guarding the heart is *warfare against the passions*. By 'passion' here is meant not just sexual lust, but any disordered appetite or longing that violently takes possession of the soul: anger, jealousy, gluttony, avarice, lust for power, pride, and the rest. Many of the Fathers treat the passions as something intrinsically evil, that is to say, as inward diseases alien to man's true nature. Some of them, however, adopt a more positive standpoint, regarding the passions as dynamic impulses originally placed in man by God, and so fundamentally good, although at present distorted by sin. On this second and more subtle view, our aim is not to eliminate the passions but to redirect their energy. Uncontrolled rage must be turned into righteous indignation, spiteful jealousy into zeal for the truth, sexual lust into an *eros* that is pure in its fervour. The passions, then, are to be purified, not killed; to be educated, not eradicated; to be used positively, not negatively. To ourselves and to others we say, not 'Suppress', but 'Transfigure'.

This effort to purify the passions needs to be carried out on the level of both soul and body. On the level of the soul they are purified through prayer, through the regular use of the sacraments of Confession and Communion, through daily reading of Scripture, through feeding our mind with the thought of what is good, through practical acts of loving service to others. On the level of the body they are purified above all through fasting and abstinence, and through frequent prostrations during the time of prayer. Knowing that man is not an angel but a unity of body and soul, the Orthodox

Church insists upon the spiritual value of bodily fasting. We do not fast because there is anything in itself unclean about the act of eating and drinking. Food and drink are on the contrary God's gift, from which we are to partake with enjoyment and gratitude. We fast, not because we despise the divine gift, but so as to make ourselves aware that it is indeed a gift — so as to purify our eating and drinking, and to make them, no longer a concession to greed, but a sacrament and means of communion with the Giver. Understood in this way, ascetic fasting is directed, not against the body, but against the flesh (pp. 79–80). Its aim is not destructively to weaken the body, but creatively to render the body more spiritual.

Purification of the passions leads eventually, by God's grace, to what Evagrius terms *apatheia* or 'dispassion'. By this he means, not a negative condition of indifference or insensitivity in which we no longer *feel* temptation, but a positive state of reintegration and spiritual freedom in which we no longer *yield* to temptation. Perhaps *apatheia* can best be translated 'purity of heart'. It signifies advancing from instability to stability, from duplicity to simplicity or singleness of heart, from the immaturity of fear and suspicion to the maturity of innocence and trust. For Evagrius dispassion and love are integrally connected, as the two sides of a coin. If you lust, you cannot love. Dispassion means that we are no longer dominated by selfishness and uncontrolled desire, and so we become capable of true love.

The 'dispassioned' person, so far from being apathetic, is the one whose heart burns with love for God, for other humans, for every living creature, for all that God has made. As St Isaac the

Syrian writes:

When a man with such a heart as this thinks of the creatures and looks at them, his eyes are filled with tears because of the overwhelming compassion that presses upon his heart. The heart of such a man grows tender, and he cannot endure to hear of or look upon any injury, even the smallest suffering, inflicted upon anything in creation. Therefore he never ceases to pray with tears even for the dumb animals, for the enemies of truth and for all who do harm to it, asking that they may be guarded and receive God's mercy. And for the reptiles also he prays with a great compassion, which rises up endlessly in his heart, after the example of God.

Through Creation to the Creator

The second stage upon the threefold Way is the contemplation of nature — more exactly, the contemplation of nature in God, or the contemplation of God in and through nature. The second stage is thus a prelude and means of entry to the third: by contemplating the things which God has made, the man of prayer is brought to the contemplation of God himself. This second stage of *physiki* or 'natural contemplation', as we have stated, is not necessarily subsequent to *praktiki* but may be simultaneous with it.

No contemplation of any kind is possible without *nepsis* or watchfulness. I cannot contemplate either nature or God without learning to be present where I am, gathered together at this present moment, in this present place. Stop, look and listen. Such is the first beginning of contemplation. The contemplation of nature commences when I open my eyes, literally and spiritually, and start to notice the world around myself — to notice the *real* world, that is to say, *God's* world. The contemplative is the one who, like Moses before the Burning Bush (Exod. 3:5), takes off his shoes — that is, strips himself of the deadness of familiarity and boredom — and who then recognizes that the place where he is standing is holy ground. To contemplate nature is to become aware of the dimensions of sacred space and sacred time. *This* material object, *this* person to whom I am talking, *this* moment of time — each is holy, each is in its own way unrepeatable and so of infinite value, each can serve as a window into eternity. And, becoming sensitive to God's world around myself, I grow more conscious also of God's world *within* myself. Beginning to see nature in God, I begin to see my own place as a human person within the natural order; I begin to understand what it is to be microcosm and mediator.

In earlier chapters we have indicated the theological basis for this contemplation of nature. All things are permeated and maintained in being by the uncreated energies of God, and so all things are a theophany that mediates his presence (pp. 27–29). At the heart of each thing is its inner principle or *logos,* implanted within it by the Creator Logos; and so through the *logoi* we enter into communion with the Logos (p. 41). God is above and beyond all things, yet as Creator he is also within all things – 'panentheism', not pantheism (p. 58). To contemplate nature, then, is in Blake's phrase to cleanse the 'doors of our perception', both on the physical and on the spiritual level, and thereby to discern the energies or *logoi* of God in everything that he has made. It is to discover, not so much through our discursive reason as through our spiritual intellect, that the whole universe is a cosmic Burning Bush, filled with the divine Fire yet not consumed.

Such is the theological basis; but the contemplation of nature requires also a moral basis. We cannot make progress on the second stage of the Way unless we make progress on the first stage by practising the virtues and fulfilling the commandments. Our natural contemplation, if it lacks a firm foundation in the 'active life', becomes merely aesthetic or romantic, and fails to rise to the level of the genuinely noetic or spiritual. There can be no perception of the world in God without radical repentance, without a continual change of mind.

The contemplation of nature has two correlative aspects. First, it means appreciating the 'thusness' or 'thisness' of particular things, persons and moments. We are to see each stone, each leaf, each blade of grass, each frog, each human face, for what it truly is, in all the distinctness and intensity of its specific being. As the prophet Zechariah warns us, we are not to 'despise the day of small things' (4:10). 'True mysticism', says Olivier Clément, 'is to discover the extraordinary in the ordinary.' No existing thing is paltry or despicable, for as God's handiwork each has its unique place in the created order. Sin alone is mean and trivial, as are most of the products of a fallen and sinful technology; but sin, as we have already noted, is not a real thing, and the products of sinfulness, despite their apparent solidity and destructive power, partake likewise of the same unreality.

Secondly, the contemplation of nature means that we see all things, persons and moments as signs and sacraments of God. In our spiritual vision we are not only to see each thing in sharp relief, standing out in all the brilliance of its specific being, but we are also to see each thing as transparent: in and through each created thing we are to discern the

Creator. Discovering the uniqueness of each thing, we discover also how each points beyond itself to him who made it. So we learn, in Henry Suso's words, to see the inward in the outward: 'He who can see the inward in the outward, to him the inward is more inward than to him who can only see the inward in the inward.'

These two aspects of natural contemplation are exactly indicated in George Herbert's poem *The Elixir:*

Teach me, my God and King,
In all things thee to see,
And what I do in any thing,
To do it as for thee.

A man that looks on glasse,
On it may stay his eye;
Or if he pleaseth, through it passe,
And then the heav'n espie.

To look *on* the glass is to perceive the 'thisness', the intense reality, of each thing; to look *through* the glass and so to 'espie' the heaven is to discern God's presence within and yet beyond that thing. These two ways of looking at the world confirm and complement one another. Creation leads us to God, and God sends us back again to creation, enabling us to look at nature with the eyes of Adam in Paradise. For, seeing all things in God, we see them with a vividness that they would never otherwise possess.

We are not to restrict God's presence in the world to a limited range of 'pious' objects and situations, while labelling everything else as 'secular'; but we are to see all things as essentially sacred, as a gift from God and a means of communion with him. It does not, however, follow that we are to accept the fallen world on its own terms. This is the unhappy mistake of much 'secular Christianity' in the contemporary west. All things are indeed sacred in their true being, according to their innermost essence; but our relationship to God's creation has been distorted by sin, original and personal, and we shall not rediscover this intrinsic sacredness unless our heart is purified. Without self-denial, without ascetic discipline, we cannot affirm the true beauty of the world. That is why there can be no genuine contemplation without repentance.

Natural contemplation signifies finding God not only in all *things* but equally in all *persons*. When reverencing the holy ikons in church or at home, we are to reflect that each man and woman is a living ikon of God. 'Inasmuch as you did it to one of the least of these my brethren, you did it to me' (Matt. 25:40). In order to find God, we do not have to leave the world, to isolate ourselves from our fellow humans, and to plunge into some kind of mystical void. On the contrary, Christ is looking at us through the eyes of all those whom we meet. Once we recognize his universal presence, all our acts of practical service to others become acts of prayer.

It is common to regard contemplation as a rare and exalted gift, and so no doubt it is in its plenitude. Yet the seeds of a contemplative attitude exist in all of us. From this hour and moment I can start to walk through the world, conscious that it is God's world, that he is near me in everything that I see and touch, in everyone whom I encounter. However spasmodically and incompletely I do this, I have already set foot upon the contemplative path.

Many people who find the imageless prayer of silence altogether beyond their present capacity, and for whom the familiar phrases written in Scripture or in the books of prayer have grown dull and dry, can renew their inward life through the practice of natural contemplation. Learning to read God's word in the book of creation, discovering his signature in all things, I then find — when I return to read his word in Scripture and the books of prayer — that the well-known phrases have a fresh depth of meaning. So nature and Scripture complement each other. In the words of St Ephrem the Syrian:

> *Wherever you turn your eyes, there is God's symbol;*
> *Wherever you read, you will find there his types. . .*
> *Look and see how Nature and Scripture are linked together. . .*
> *Praise for the Lord of Nature,*
> *Glory for the Lord of Scripture.*

From Words to Silence

The more a man comes to contemplate God in nature, the more he realizes that God is also above and beyond nature. Finding traces of the divine in all things, he says: 'This also is thou; neither is this thou.' So the second stage of the spiritual Way leads him, with God's help, to the third stage, when God is no longer known solely through the medium of what he has made but in direct and unmediated union.

The transition from the second to the third level is effected, so we learn from our spiritual masters in the Orthodox tradition, by applying to the life of prayer the way of negation or apophatic approach (see p. 16). In Scripture, in the liturgical texts, and in nature, we are presented with innumerable words, images and symbols of God; and we are taught to give full value to these words, images and symbols, dwelling upon them in our prayer. But, since these things can never express the entire truth about the living God, we are encouraged also to balance this affirmative or cataphatic prayer by apophatic prayer. As Evagrius puts it, 'Prayer is a laying aside of thoughts.' This is not of course to be regarded as a complete definition of prayer, but it does indicate the kind of prayer that leads a man from the second to the third stage of the Way. Reaching out towards the eternal Truth that lies beyond all human words and thoughts, the seeker begins to wait upon God in quietness and silence, no longer talking about or to God but simply listening. 'Be still, and know that I am God' (Ps. 46:10).

This stillness or inward silence is known in Greek as *hesychia*, and he who seeks the prayer of stillness is termed a hesychast. *Hesychia* signifies concentration combined with inward tranquillity. It is not merely to be understood in a negative sense as the absence of speech and outward activity, but it denotes in a positive way the openness of the human heart towards God's love. Needless to say, for most people if not all, *hesychia* is not a permanent state. The hesychast, as well as entering into the prayer of stillness, uses other forms of prayer as well, sharing in corporate liturgical worship, reading Scripture, receiving the sacraments. Apophatic prayer coexists with cataphatic, and each strengthens the other. The way of negation and the way of affirmation are not alternatives; they are complementary.

But how are we to stop talking and to start listening? Of all the lessons in prayer, this is the hardest to learn. There is little profit in saying to ourselves, 'Do not think', for suspension of discursive thought is not something that we can achieve merely through an exertion of will-power. The ever-restless mind demands from us some task, so as to satisfy its constant need to be active. If our spiritual strategy is entirely negative — if we try to eliminate all conscious thinking without offering our mind any alternative activity — we are likely to end up with vague day-dreaming. The mind needs some task which will keep it busy, and yet enable it to reach out beyond itself into stillness. In the Orthodox hesychast tradition, the work which is usually assigned to it is the frequent repetition of some short 'arrow prayer', most commonly the Jesus Prayer: *Lord Jesus Christ, Son of God, have mercy on me a sinner.*

We are taught, when reciting the Jesus Prayer, to avoid so far as possible any specific image or picture. In the words of St Gregory of Nyssa, 'The Bridegroom is present, but he is not seen.' The Jesus Prayer is not a form of imaginative meditation upon different incidents in the life of Christ. But, while turning aside from images, we are to concentrate our full attention upon, or rather within, the words. The Jesus Prayer is not just a hypnotic incantation but a meaningful phrase, an invocation addressed to another Person. Its object is not relaxation but alertness, not waking slumber but living prayer. And so the Jesus Prayer is not to be said mechanically but with inward purpose; yet at the same time the words should be pronounced without tension, violence, or undue emphasis. The string round our spiritual parcel should be taut, not left hanging slack; yet it should not be drawn so tight as to cut into the edges of the package.

Normally three levels or degrees are distinguished in the saying of the Jesus Prayer. It starts as 'prayer of the lips', oral prayer. Then it grows more inward, becoming 'prayer of the intellect', mental prayer. Finally the intellect 'descends' into the heart and is united with it, and so the prayer becomes 'prayer of the heart' or, more exactly, 'prayer of the intellect in the heart'. At this level it becomes prayer of the whole person — no longer something that we think or say, but something that we are: for the ultimate purpose of the spiritual Way is not just a person who *says* prayers from time to time, but a person who *is* prayer all the time. The Jesus Prayer, that is to say, begins as a series of specific *acts* of prayer, but its eventual aim is to establish in the one who prays a *state* of prayer that is unceasing, which continues uninterrupted even in the midst of other activities.

So the Jesus Prayer begins as an oral prayer like any other. But the rhythmic repetition of the same short phrase enables the hesychast, by virtue of the very simplicity of the words which he uses, to advance beyond all language and images into the mystery of God. In this way the Jesus Prayer develops, with God's help, into what Western writers call 'prayer of loving attention' or 'prayer of simple gaze', where the soul rests in God without a constantly varying succession of images, ideas and feelings. Beyond this there is a further stage, when the hesychast's prayer ceases to be the result of his own efforts, and becomes — at any rate from time to time — what Orthodox writers call 'self-acting' and Western writers call 'infused'. It ceases, in other words, to be 'my' prayer, and becomes to a greater or lesser extent the prayer of *Christ in me*.

Yet it is not to be imagined that this transition from oral prayer to prayer of silence, or from 'active' to 'self-acting' prayer, is rapidly and easily made. The anonymous author of *The Way of a Pilgrim* was granted continual 'self-acting' prayer after only a few weeks of practising the Invocation of the Name of Jesus, but his case is altogether most exceptional and should on no account be regarded as the norm. More commonly, those who recite the Jesus Prayer are granted from time to time moments of 'rapture', coming unexpectedly as a free gift, when the words of prayer recede into the background or disappear altogether, and are replaced by an immediate sense of God's presence and love. But for the great majority this experience is only a brief glimpse, not a continuous state. It would in any case be most unwise to attempt to induce by artificial means what can only come about as the fruit of God's direct action. The best course, when invoking the Holy Name, is to concentrate our full efforts upon the recitation of the words; otherwise, in our premature attempts to attain wordless prayer of the heart, we may find that we end up by not really praying at all, but merely sitting half-asleep. Let us follow the advice of St John Climacus, 'Confine your mind within the words of prayer.' God will do the rest, but in his own way and at his own time.

Union with God

The apophatic method, whether in our theological discourse or in our life of prayer, is seemingly negative in character, but in its final aim it is supremely positive. The laying aside of thoughts and images leads not to vacuity but to a plenitude surpassing all that the human mind can conceive or express. The way of negation resembles not so much the peeling of an onion as the carving of a statue. When we peel an onion, we remove one skin after another, until finally there is no more onion left: we end up with nothing at all. But the sculptor, when chipping away at a block of marble, negates to a positive effect. He does not reduce the block to a heap of random fragments but, through the apparently destructive action of breaking the stone in pieces, he ends up by unveiling an intelligible shape.

So it is on a higher level with our use of apophaticism. We deny in order to affirm. We say that something *is not* in order to say that something *is*. The way of negation turns out to be the way of super-affirmation. Our laying aside of words and concepts serves as a spring-board or trampoline, from which we leap into the divine mystery. Apophatic theology, in its true and full meaning, leads not to an absence but to a presence, not to agnosticism but to a union of love. Thus apophatic theology is much more than a purely verbal exercise, whereby we balance positive statements with negations. Its aim is to bring us to a direct meeting with a personal God, who infinitely surpasses everything that we can say of him, whether negative or positive.

This union of love which constitutes the true aim of the apophatic approach is a union with God in his energies, not in his essence (see pp. 27–28). Bearing in mind what has been said earlier about the Trinity and the Incarnation, it is possible to distinguish three different kinds of union:

First, there is between the three persons of the Trinity a union *according to essence*: Father, Son and Holy Spirit are 'one in essence'. But between God and the saints no such union takes place. Although 'ingodded' or 'deified', the saints do not become additional members of the Trinity. God remains God, and man remains man. Man becomes god by grace, but not God in essence. The distinction between Creator and creature still continues: it is bridged by mutual love but not abolished. God, however near he draws to man, still remains the 'Wholly Other'.

Secondly, there is between the divine and the human natures of the incarnate Christ a union *according to hypostasis,* a 'hypostatic' or personal union: Godhead and manhood in Christ are so joined that they constitute, or belong to, a single person. Once more, the union between God and the saints is not of this kind. In the mystical union between God and the soul, there are two persons, not one (or, more exactly, four persons: one human person, and the three divine persons of the undivided Trinity). It is an 'I — Thou' relationship: the 'Thou' still remains 'Thou', however close the 'I' may draw near. The saints are plunged into the abyss of divine love, yet not swallowed up. 'Christification' does not signify annihilation. In the Age to come God is 'all in all' (1 Cor. 15:28); but 'Peter is Peter, Paul is Paul, Philip is Philip. Each one retains his own nature and personal identity, but they are all filled with the Spirit' (*The Homilies of St Macarius*).

Since, then, the union between God and the human beings that he has created is a union neither according to essence nor according to hypostasis, it remains thirdly that it should be a union *according to energy.* The saints do not become God by essence nor one person with God, but they participate in the energies of God, that is to say, in his life, power, grace and glory. The energies, as we have insisted, are not to be 'objectified' or regarded as an intermediary between God and man, a 'thing' or gift which God bestows on his creation. The energies are truly *God himself* — yet not God as he exists *within* himself, in his inner life, but God as he communicates himself in outgoing love. He who participates in God's energies is therefore meeting God himself face to face, through a direct and personal union of love, in so far as a created being is capable of this. To say that man participates in the energies but not in the essence of God is to say that between man and God there is brought to pass union but not confusion. It means that we affirm concerning God, in the most literal and emphatic way, 'His life is mine', while at the same time repudiating pantheism. We assert God's nearness, while at the same time proclaiming his otherness.

Darkness and Light

In referring to this 'union according to energy', which lies far beyond all that man can imagine or describe, the saints have perforce used the language of paradox and symbolism. For human speech is adapted to delineate that which exists in space and time, and even here it can never provide an exhaustive description. As for what is infinite and eternal, here human speech can do no more than point or hint.

The two chief 'signs' or symbols employed by Fathers are those of darkness and light. Not, of course, that God as such is either light or darkness: we are speaking in parables or analogies. According to their preference for the one 'sign' or the other, mystical writers may be characterized as either 'nocturnal' or 'solar'. St Clement of Alexandria (drawing on the Jewish author Philo), St Gregory of Nyssa and St Dionysius the Areopagite give preference to the 'sign' of darkness;

Origen, St Gregory the Theologian, Evagrius, *The Homilies of St Macarius,* St Symeon the New Theologian and St Gregory Palamas use chiefly the 'sign' of light.

'Darkness' language, as applied to God, takes its origin chiefly from the Biblical description of Moses upon Mount Sinai, when he is said to enter into the 'thick darkness' where God was (Exod. 20:21: compare p. 15). It is significant that in his passage it is not stated that God *is* darkness, but that he *dwells* in darkness: the darkness denotes, not the absence or unreality of God, but the inability of our human mind to grasp God's inner nature. The darkness is in us, and not in him.

The primary basis for 'light' language is the sentence in St John, 'God is light, and in him is no darkness at all' (1 John 1:5). God is revealed as light above all at the Transfiguration of Christ on Mount Tabor, when 'his face shone as the sun, and his raiment was white as the light' (Matt. 17:2). This divine light, seen by the three disciples on the mountain — seen also by many of the saints during prayer — is nothing else than the uncreated energies of God. The light of Tabor, that is to say, is neither a physical and created light, nor yet a purely metaphorical 'light of the intellect'. Although nonmaterial, it is nevertheless an objectively existent reality. Being divine, the uncreated energies surpass our human powers of description; and so, in terming these energies 'light', we are inevitably employing the language of 'sign' and symbol. Not that the energies are themselves merely symbolical. They genuinely exist, but cannot be described in words; in referring to them as 'light' we use the least misleading term, but our language is not to be interpreted literally.

Although non-physical, the divine light can be seen by a man through his physical eyes, provided that his senses have been transformed by divine grace. His eyes do not behold the light by the natural powers of perception, but through the power of the Holy Spirit acting within him.

'The body is deified at the same time as the soul' (St Maximus the Confessor). He who beholds the divine light is permeated by it through and through, so that his body shines with the glory that he contemplates. He himself becomes light. Vladimir Lossky was not speaking merely in metaphors when he wrote: 'The fire of grace, kindled in the hearts of Christians by the Holy Spirit, makes them shine like tapers before the Son of God.' *The Homilies of St Macarius* affirm concerning this transfiguration of man's body:

Just as the Lord's body was glorified, when he went up the mountain and was transfigured into the glory of God and into infinite light, so the saints' bodies also are glorified and shine as lightning. . . 'The glory which thou hast given to me I have given to them' (John 17:22): just as many lamps are lit from one flame, so the bodies of the saints, being members of Christ, must needs be what Christ is, and nothing else. . . Our human nature is transformed into the power of God, and it is kindled into fire and light.

In the lives of the saints, Western as well as Eastern, there are numerous examples of such bodily glorification. When Moses came down from the darkness of Sinai, his face shone with such brilliance that no one could gaze upon it, and he had to place a veil over it when talking with others (Exod. 34:29–35). In *The Sayings of the Desert Fathers* we are told how a disciple looked through the window of Abba Arsenius' cell, and saw the old man 'like a flame of fire'. Of Abba Pambo it is said, 'God so glorified him that no one could look at his face, because of the glory which his face had.' Fourteen hundred years later, Nicolas Motovilov uses these words to describe a conversation with his *starets* St Seraphim of Sarov: 'Imagine in the centre of the sun, in the dazzling brilliance of its mid-day rays, the face of a man talking to you.'·

In some writers the ideas of light and darkness are combined. Henry Vaughan speaks of a 'dazzling darkness' in God, while St Dionysius uses the phrase 'radiance of divine Darkness' (p. 31). Elsewhere St Dionysius says, 'The divine darkness is the. inaccessible light in which God is said to dwell.' There is no self-contradiction about such language, for to God 'the darkness and the light are both alike' (Ps. 139:12). As Jacob Boehme puts it, 'The darkness is not the absence of light, but the terror that comes from the blinding light.' If God is said to dwell in darkness, that does not mean that there is in God any lack or privation, but that he is a fullness of glory and love beyond our comprehension.

Prayer is the test of everything. If prayer is right, everything is right.

Bishop Theophan the Recluse

'Draw nigh to God, and he will draw nigh to you' (James 4:8). It is for us to begin. If we take one step towards the Lord, he takes ten toward us — he who saw the prodigal son while he was yet at a distance, and had compassion and ran and embraced him.

Tito Colliander

The further the soul advances, the greater are the adversaries against which it must contend.

Blessed are you, if the struggle grows fierce against you at the time of prayer.

Do not think that you have acquired any virtue before you have shed your blood in your struggle for it. Until death you must fight against sin, resisting with all your strength.

Do not allow your eyes to sleep or your eyelids to slumber until the hour of your death, but labour without ceasing that you may enjoy life without end.

Evagrius of Pontus

A monk was once asked: What do you do there in the monastery? He replied: We fall and get up, fall and get up, fall and get up again.

Tito Colliander

Unless a man gives himself entirely to the Cross, in a spirit of humility and self-abasement; unless he casts himself down to be trampled underfoot by all and despised, accepting injustice, contempt and mockery; unless he undergoes all these things with joy for the sake of the Lord, not claiming any kind of human reward whatsoever — glory or honour or pleasures of food and drink and clothing — he cannot become a true Christian.

St Mark the Monk

If you would be victorious, taste the suffering of Christ in your person, that you may be chosen to taste his glory. For if we suffer with him, we shall also be glorified with him. The intellect cannot be glorified with Jesus, if the body does not suffer for Jesus.

Blessed are you if you suffer for righteousness'

sake. Behold, for years and generations the way of God has been made smooth through the Cross and by death. The way to God is a daily Cross.

The Cross is the gate of mysteries.

St Isaac the Syrian

To be 'dispassioned', passionless — in the Patristic and not the Stoic sense of the word — takes time and hard work, with austere living, fasting and vigils, prayer, sweat of blood, humiliation, the world's contempt, crucifixion, the nails, the spear in the side, vinegar and gall, being forsaken by everyone, insults from foolish brethren crucified with us, blasphemies from the passers-by: and then — resurrection in the Lord, the immortal holiness of Easter.

Fr Theoklitos of Dionysiou

Pray simply. Do not expect to find in your heart any remarkable gift of prayer. Consider yourself unworthy of it. Then you will find peace. Use the empty, cold dryness of your prayer as food for your humility. Repeat constantly: I am not worthy, Lord, I am not worthy! But say it calmly, without agitation. This humble prayer will be acceptable to God.

When practising the Jesus Prayer, remember that the most important thing of all is humility; then the ability — not the decision only — always to maintain a keen sense of responsibility towards God, towards one's spiritual director, men, and even things. Remember, too, that Isaac the Syrian warns us that God's wrath visits all who refuse the bitter cross of agony, the cross of active suffering, and who, striving after visions and special graces of prayer, waywardly seek to appropriate the glories of the Cross. He also says, 'God's grace comes of itself, suddenly, without our seeing it approach. It comes when the place is clean.' Therefore, carefully, diligently, constantly clean the place; sweep it with the broom of humility.

Starets Makarii of Optino

When we have blocked all its outlets by means of the remembrance of God, the intellect requires of us imperatively some task which will satisfy its need for activity. For the complete fulfilment of its purpose we should give it nothing but the prayer 'Lord Jesus'. Let the intellect continually concentrate on these words within its inner shrine with such intensity that it is not turned aside to any mental images.

Just as a mother teaches her baby the name 'father' and makes the child repeat the word with her again and again, until she brings it to use this name rather than any other childish cry, so that even when asleep it calls aloud to its father: so must the soul learn to repeat and to cry out 'Lord Jesus'.

St Diadochus of Photike

The Jesus Prayer helps to lift the whole life, body and soul, to a level where the senses and imagination no longer seek for outward change or stimulation, where all is subordinated to the one aim of centring the whole attention of body and soul upon God, in the sense that the world is sought and known in the beauty of God, not God in the beauty of the world.

Mother Maria of Normanby

What now is meant by Moses entering the darkness and so seeing God within it?

The text of Scripture is here teaching us that, as the intellect makes progress and by a greater and more perfect attention comes to understand what the knowledge of reality is, the more it approaches to

*contemplation, the more it sees that the divine nature
cannot be contemplated. For, leaving behind every
external appearance, not only those that can be
grasped by the senses but also those that the reason
believes itself to see, it advances continually towards
that which lies further within, until by the activity of
the mind it penetrates into that which cannot be
contemplated or comprehended; and it is there that it
sees God. The true knowledge and the true vision of
what we seek consist precisely in this — in not seeing:
for what we seek transcends all knowledge, and is
everywhere cut off from us by the darkness of
incomprehensibility.*

St Gregory of Nyssa

*In mystical contemplation a man sees neither with
the intellect nor with the body, but with the Spirit;
and with full certainty he knows that he beholds
supernaturally a light which surpasses all other light.
But he does not know through what organ he
beholds this light, nor can he analyse the nature of
the organ; for the ways of the Spirit, through which
he sees, are unsearchable. And this is what St Paul
affirmed, when he heard things which it is not lawful
for man to utter and saw things which none can
behold: '. . . whether in the body or whether out of
the body, I cannot tell' (2 Cor. 12:3) — that is, he did
not know whether it was his intellect or his body
which saw them. For he did not perceive these things
by sensation, yet his vision was as clear as that whereby we see the objects of sense perception, and even
clearer still. He saw himself carried out of himself
through the mysterious sweetness of his vision; he
was transported not only outside every object and
thought but even outside himself.*

This happy and joyful experience which seized

upon Paul and caused his intellect to pass beyond all things in ecstasy, which made him turn entirely in upon himself, this experience took the form of light — a light of revelation, but such as did not reveal to him the objects of sense perception. It was a light without bounds or termination below or above or to the sides; he saw no limit whatever to the light which appeared to him and shone around him, but it was like a sun infinitely brighter and larger than the universe: and in the midst of this light he himself stood, having become nothing but eye. Such, more or less, was his vision.

St Gregory Palamas

When the soul is counted worthy to enjoy communion with the Spirit of the light of God, and when God shines upon her with the beauty of his ineffable glory, preparing her as a throne and dwelling for himself, she becomes all light, all face, all eye; and there is no part of her that is not full of the spiritual eyes of light. There is no part of her that is in darkness, but she is made wholly and in every part light and spirit.

The Homilies of St Macarius

GOD AS ETERNITY

Lord, remember me when thou comest into thy kingdom.

Luke 23:42

To all souls that love God, to all true Christians, there shall come a first month of the year, as the month of April, a day of resurrection.

The Homilies of St Macarius

When Abba Zacharias was on the point of dying, Abba Moses asked him: 'What do you see?' And Abba Zacharias replied, 'Is it not better to say nothing, father?' 'Yes, my child,' said Abba Moses, 'it is better to say nothing.'

The Sayings of the Desert Fathers

Speech is the organ of this present world. Silence is the mystery of the world to come.

St Isaac the Syrian

The End draws near

'I am waiting for the resurrection of the dead and the life of the Age to come.' Oriented towards the future, the Creed ends upon a note of expectation. But, although the Last Things should form our point of constant reference throughout this earthly life, it is not possible for us to speak in any detail about the realities of the Age to come. 'Beloved', writes St John, 'now we are the children of God; but it has not yet been made clear to us what we shall be' (1 John 3:2). Through our faith in Christ, we possess here and now a living, personal relationship with God; and we know, not as a hypothesis but as a present fact of experience, that this relationship already contains within itself the seeds of eternity. But what it is like to live not within the time sequence but in the eternal *Now,* not under the conditions of the fall but in a universe where God is 'all in all' — of this we have only partial glimpses but no clear conception; and so we should speak always .with caution, respecting the need for silence.

There are, however, at least three things that we are entitled to affirm without ambiguity: that Christ will come again in glory; that at his coming we shall be raised from the dead and judged; and that 'of his kingdom there shall be no end' (Luke 1:33).

First, then, Scripture and Holy Tradition speak to us repeatedly about the Second Coming. They give us no grounds for supposing that, through a steady advance in 'civilization', the world will grow gradually better and better until mankind succeeds in establishing God's kingdom upon earth. The Christian view of world history is entirely opposed to this kind of evolutionary optimism. What we are taught to expect are disasters in the world of nature, increasingly destructive warfare between men, bewilderment and apostasy among those who call themselves Christians (see especially Matt. 24:3-27). This period of tribulation will culminate with the appearance of 'the man of sin' (2 Thess. 2:3-4) or Antichrist, who, according to the interpretation traditional in the Orthodox Church, will not be Satan himself, but a human being, a genuine man, in whom all the forces of evil will be concentrated and who will for a time hold the entire world under his sway. The brief reign of Antichrist will be abruptly terminated by the Second Coming of the Lord, this time not in a hidden way, as at his birth in Bethlehem, but 'sitting on the right hand of power, and drawing near upon the clouds of heaven' (Matt. 26:64). So the course of history will be brought to a sudden and dramatic end, through a direct intervention from the divine realm.

The precise time of the Second Coming is hidden from us: 'It is not for you to know the times and the seasons, which the Father has determined by his own decision' (Acts 1:7). The Lord will come 'as a thief in the night' (1 Thess. 5:2). This means that, while avoiding speculation about the exact date, we are to be always prepared and expectant. 'What I say unto you I say unto all: Watch' (Mark 13:37). For, whether the End comes late or soon in our human time-scale, it is always *imminent*, always spiritually close at hand. We are to have in our hearts a sense of urgency. In the words of the Great Canon of St Andrew of Crete, recited each Lent:

> *My soul, O my soul, rise up! Why art thou sleeping?*
> *The End draws near, and soon shalt thou be troubled.*
> *Watch, then, that Christ thy God may spare thee,*
> *For he is everywhere present and fills all things.*

The Future Springtime

Secondly, as Christians we believe not only in the immortality of the soul but in the resurrection of the body. According to God's ordinance at our first creation, the human soul and the human body are interdependent, and neither can properly exist without the other. In consequence of the fall, the two are parted at bodily death, but this separation is not final and permanent. At the Second Coming of Christ, we shall be raised from the dead in our soul and in our body; and so, with soul and body reunited, we shall appear before our Lord for the Last Judgement.

Judgement, as St John's Gospel emphasizes, is going on all the time throughout our earthly existence. Whenever, consciously or unconsciously, we choose the good, we enter already by anticipation into eternal life; whenever we choose evil, we receive a foretaste of hell. The Last Judgement is best understood as the *moment of truth* when everything is brought to light, when all our acts of choice stand revealed to us in their full implications, when we realize with absolute clarity who we are and what has been the deep meaning and aim of our life. And so, following this final clarification, we shall enter — with soul and body reunited — into heaven or hell, into eternal life or eternal death.

Christ is the judge; and yet, from another point of view, it is we who pronounce judgement upon ourselves. If anyone is in hell, it is not because God has imprisoned him there, but because that is where he himself has chosen to be. The lost in hell are self-condemned, self-enslaved; it has been rightly said that the doors of hell are locked *on the inside.*

How can a God of love accept that even a single one of the creatures whom he has made should remain for ever in hell? There is a mystery here which, from our standpoint in this present life, we cannot hope to fathom. The best we can do is to hold in balance two truths, contrasting but not contradictory. First, God has given free will to man, and so to all eternity it lies in man's power to reject God. Secondly, love signifies compassion, involvement; and so, if there are any who remain eternally in hell, in some sense God is also there with them. It is written in the Psalms, 'If I go down to hell, thou art there also' (139:7); and St Isaac the Syrian says, 'It is wrong to imagine that sinners in hell are cut off from the love of God.' Divine love is everywhere, and rejects no one. But we on our side are free to reject divine love: we cannot, however, do so without inflicting pain upon ourselves, and the more final our rejection the more bitter our suffering.

'At the resurrection', state *The Homilies of St Macarius,* 'all the members of the body are raised: not a hair perishes' (compare Luke 21:18). At the same time the resurrection body is said to be a 'spiritual body' (see 1 Cor. 15:35-46). This does not mean that at the resurrection our bodies will be somehow dematerialized; but we are to remember that matter as we know it in this fallen world, with all its inertness and opacity, does not at all correspond to matter as God intended it to be. Freed from the grossness of the fallen flesh, the resurrection body will share in the qualities of Christ's human body at the Transfiguration and after the Resurrection. But, although transformed, our resurrection body will still be in a recognizable way the same body as that which we have now: there will be continuity between the two. In the words of St Cyril of Jerusalem:

It is this selfsame body that is raised, although not in its present state of weakness; for it will 'put on incorruption' (1 Cor. 15:53) and so be transformed. . . It will no longer need the foods which we now eat to keep it alive, nor stairs for its ascent; for it will be made spiritual and will become something marvel-

lous, such as we cannot properly describe.

And St Irenaeus testifies:

Neither the structure nor the substance of creation is destroyed. It is only the 'outward form of this world' (1 Cor. 7:31) that passes away — that is to say, the conditions produced by the fall. And when this 'outward form' has passed away, man will be renewed and will flourish in a prime of life that is incorruptible, so that it is no longer possible for him to grow old any more. There will be 'a new heaven and a new earth' (Rev. 21:1); and in this new heaven and new earth man shall abide, for ever new and for ever conversing with God.

'A new heaven and a new earth': man is not saved *from* his body but *in* it; not saved *from* the material world but *with* it. Because man is microcosm and mediator of the creation, his own salvation involves also the reconciliation and transfiguration of the whole animate and inanimate creation around him — its deliverance 'from the bondage of corruption' and entry 'into the glorious liberty of the children of God' (Rom. 8:21). In the 'new earth' of the Age to come there is surely a place not only for man but for the animals: in and through man, they too will share in immortality, and so will rocks, trees and plants, fire and water.

A Journey into the Infinite

This resurrection kingdom, in which we shall by God's mercy dwell with our soul and body reunited, is in the third place a kingdom which shall have 'no end'. Its eternity and infinity are beyond the scope of our fallen imagination, but of two things at any rate we may be sure. First, perfection is not uniform but diversified. Secondly, perfection is not static but dynamic.

First, eternity signifies an inexhaustible variety. If it is true of our experience in this life that holiness is not monotonous but always different, must this not be true also, and to an incomparably higher degree, of the future life? God promises to us: 'To him that overcomes will I give . . . a white stone, and on the stone a new name written, which no man knows except the one who receives it' (Rev. 2:17). Even in the Age to come, the inner meaning of my unique personhood will continue to be eternally a secret between God and me. In God's kingdom each is one with all the others, yet each is distinctively himself, bearing the same delineaments as he had in this life, yet with these characteristics healed, renewed and glorified. In the words of St Isaias of Sketis:

The Lord Jesus in his mercy grants rest to each according to his works — to the great according to his greatness and to the little according to his littleness; for he said, 'In my Father's house are many mansions' (John 14:2). Though the kingdom is one, yet in the one kingdom each finds his own special place and his own special work.

Secondly, eternity signifies unending progress, a never-ceasing advance. As J.R.R. Tolkien has said, 'Roads go ever ever on'. This is true of the spiritual Way, not only in the present life, but also in the Age to come. We move constantly onwards. And it is *forward* that we go, not back. The Age to come is not simply a return to the beginning, a restoration of the original state of perfection in Paradise, but it is a fresh departure. There is to be a *new* heaven and a *new* earth; and the last things will be greater than the first.

'Here below', says Newman, 'to live is to change, and to be perfect is to have changed often.' But is this the case only here below? St Gregory of Nyssa believed that even in heaven perfection is growth. In a fine paradox he says that the essence of perfection consists precisely in never becoming perfect, but in always reaching forward to some higher perfection that lies beyond. Because God is infinite, this constant 'reaching forward' or *epektasis*, as the Greek Fathers termed it, proves limitless. The soul possesses God, and yet still seeks him; her joy is full, and yet grows always more intense. God grows ever nearer to us, yet he still remains the Other; we behold him face to face, yet we still continue to advance further and further into the divine mystery. Although strangers no longer, we do not cease to be pilgrims. We go forward 'from glory to glory' (2 Cor. 3:18), and then to a glory that is greater still. Never, in all eternity, shall we reach a point where we have accomplished all that there is to do, or discovered all that there is to know. 'Not only in this present age but also in the Age to come', says St Irenaeus, 'God will always have something more to teach man, and man will always have something more to learn from God.'

AUTHORS AND SOURCES

(I)
ORTHODOX

Andrew of Crete, St (c. 660-740): Greek bishop and hymno-grapher, author of *The Great Canon* (to be found in *The Lenten Triodion*).

Antony of Egypt, St (c. 251-356): hermit and monastic pioneer; *Life,* by St Athanasius, tr. R.T. Meyer (Ancient Christian Writers, vol.x: Washington, 1965).

Antony (Khrapovitsky), Metropolitan of Kiev (1863-1936): Russian theologian, first primate of the Russian Orthodox Church in Exile. Author of *Confession. A Series of Lectures on the Mystery of Repentance* (Jordanville, N.Y., 1975), *etc.*

Aphrahat (early 4th century): the first Syriac Father.

Athanasius of Alexandria, St (c. 296-373): Greek Father, opponent of Arianism. His best known work is *On the Incarnation,* tr. R.W. Thomson (Oxford, 1971).

Augustine, St (354-430): Bishop of Hippo, Latin Father, author of the *Confessions.*

Basil the Great, St (c. 330-79): Archbishop of Caesarea; Greek Father, one of the three 'Great Hierarchs', brother of St Gregory of Nyssa. See W.K. Lowther Clarke, *The Ascetic Works of Saint Basil* (London, 1925), *etc.*

Beausobre, Iulia de (Lady Namier) (1893-1977): Russian writer, author of *The Woman who could not Die* (London, 1938) and *Creative Suffering* (London, 1940).

Berdyaev, Nicolas (1874-1948): Russian religious philosopher, author of *The Destiny of Man* (London, 1937), *The Meaning of the Creative Act* (London, 1955), *etc.*

Bulgakov, Archpriest Sergius (1871-1944), Russian theologian, dean of the Orthodox Theological Institute of St Sergius in Paris, author of *The Orthodox Church* (London, 1935). See J. Pain and N. Zernov (edd.), *A Bulgakov Anthology* (London, 1976).

Clement of Alexandria, St (c.150 - c.215): Greek Father. Author of *Exhortation to the Greeks*, tr. G.W. Butterworth (The Loeb Classical Library, Cambridge, Mass., 1919).

Clément, Olivier (born 1921): French Orthodox writer; author of *Questions sur l'homme* (Paris, 1972) and *The Spirit of Solzhenitsyn* (London, 1976).

Colliander, Tito (born 1904): member of the Orthodox Church of Finland, writer and teacher, author of *The Way of the Ascetics* (London, 1960).

Cyril of Alexandria, St (died 444): Greek Father, noted for his devotion to the Virgin Mary, whom he honoured with the title 'Theotokos'.

Cyril of Jerusalem, St (c. 315-86): Greek Father, author of *Lectures on the Christian Sacraments*, tr. F.L. Cross (London, 1951; St Vladimir's Seminary Press, New York, 1977).

Diadochus of Photike, St (mid 5th century): Greek spiritual writer. His chief work appears in *The Philokalia*, tr. G.E.H. Palmer, P. Sherrard and K. Ware, vol.i (London, 1979).

Dimitrii of Rostov, St (1651-1709): Russian bishop, celebrated as a preacher and writer.

Dionysius the Areopagite, St (c. 500): Greek mystical theologian; author of *The Divine Names* and *The Mystical Theology*, tr. C.E. Rolt (London, 1920).

Dostoevsky, Feodor (1821-81): Russian novelist. The figure of *Starets* Zosima, in the novel *The Brothers Karamazov*, is based in part upon St Tikhon of Zadonsk and Fr Ambrose of Optino.

Elchaninov, Archpriest Alexander (1881-1934): priest of the Russian emigration in France, author of *The Diary of a Russian*

Priest (London, 1967).

Ephrem the Syrian, St (c. 306–73): Syriac Father. For a selection of his hymns, see S. Brock, *The Harp of the Spirit* (Fellowship of St Alban and St Sergius, London, 1975).

Eriúgena, John Scotus (c. 810-c. 877): Irish scholar and philosopher.

Evágrius of Pontus (346–99): monk at Sketis in Egypt, ascetical* and mystical writer. His *153 Texts on Prayer* are included in *The Philokalia,* vol. i (London, 1979).

Evdokimov, Paul (1901–70): Russian lay theologian, professor at the Orthodox Theological Institute of St Sergius in Paris; author of *L'Orthodoxie* (Paris, 1959), *The Struggle with God* (Paulist Press, N.Y., 1966), *etc.*

Festal Menaion, The: Orthodox service book containing the texts for Christmas, Epiphany and other fixed feasts in the annual calendar. Eng. tr. by Mother Mary and Archimandrite Kallistos Ware (London, 1969).

Florovsky, Archpriest George (born 1893): theologian of the Russian emigration. Four volumes of his *Collected Works* have so far appeared (Nordland Publishing Company, Belmont, Mass., 1972–6).

Gregory of Nyssa, St (c. 330 – c. 395): Greek Father. Extracts from his writings: *From Glory to Glory,* ed. J. Daniélou and H. Musurillo (London, 1962; St Vladimir's Seminary Press, New York, 1979).

Gregory Palamas, St (1296–1359): Archbishop of Thessalonica, Greek Father, defender of the Hesychast tradition of prayer. See J. Meyendorff, *A Study of Gregory Palamas* (London, 1964; St Vladimir's Seminary Press, New York, 1974) and *St Gregory Palamas and Orthodox Spirituality* (St Vladimir's Seminary Press, New York, 1974).

Gregory the Theologian, St (329–89): commonly known in the west as 'Gregory of Nazianzus', one of the three 'Great Hierarchs'. His celebrated *Theological Orations* may be found in Eng. tr. in *Nicene and Post-Nicene Fathers,* second series, vol. vii (Oxford, 1894).

Hermas (2nd century): author of *The Shepherd*, to be found in J.B. Lightfoot (tr.), *The Apostolic Fathers* (London, 1891).

Ignatii (Brianchaninov), Bishop (1807–67): Russian spiritual writer, author of *On the Prayer of Jesus* (London, 1952) and *The Arena* (Madras, 1970), both translated by Archimandrite Lazarus (Moore).

Ioannikios, St (c. 754 – c. 846): Greek ascetic, monk at Mount Olympus in Asia Minor, opponent of the Iconoclasts.

Irenaeus of Lyons, St (c. 130 – c. 200): Greek Father, a native of Asia Minor; knew St Polycarp of Smyrna; in later life Bishop of Lyons. Besides a long work *Against the Heresies,* he wrote a short *Demonstration of the Apostolic Preaching,* tr. J.A. Robinson (London, 1920).

Isaac the Syrian, St (late 7th century): Bishop of Nineveh, Syriac Father. His *Mystic Treatises* are tr. by A.J. Wensinck (Amsterdam, 1923).

Isaias of Sketis, St (died 489): Greek monk, first in Egypt and subsequently in Palestine.

John Chrysostom, St (c. 347–407): Archbishop of Constantinople, Greek Father, one of the three 'Great Hierarchs'. The best known of his many writings is *On the Priesthood,* tr. G. Neville (London, 1964; St Vladimir's Seminary Press, New York, 1977).

John Climacus, St (?579–?649): also known as 'John of the Ladder'; Greek spiritual writer, abbot of Sinai, author of *The Ladder of Divine Ascent,* tr. Archimandrite Lazarus (Moore) (London, 1959).

John of Damascus, St (c.675–c.749): Greek Father, hymn-writer, opponent of the Iconoclasts. Author of *The Exact Description of the Orthodox Faith,* Eng. tr. in *Nicene and Post-Nicene Fathers,* second series, vol.ix (Oxford, 1899).

John of Kronstadt, St (1829-1908): Russian priest, a member of the married parish clergy. See W. Jardine Grisbrooke (ed.), *Spiritual Counsels of Father John of Kronstadt* (London, 1967).

Kallistos Kataphygiotis (?14th century): Greek spiritual writer.

Khomiakov, Aleksei (1804–60): Russian lay theologian, leader of the Slavophil movement. For his essay, *The Church is One* and some of his letters, see W.J. Birkbeck (ed.), *Russia and the English Church* (London, 1895). See also A. Schmemann (ed.), *Ultimate Questions* (London/Oxford, 1977; St Vladimir's Seminary Press, New York, 1977).

Lenten Triodion, The: Orthodox service book used in the ten weeks before Easter. Eng. tr. by Mother Mary and Archimandrite Kallistos Ware (London, 1978).

Leontius of Cyprus, St (6th–7th century): Greek Father, defender of the holy ikons.

Lossky, Vladimir (1903–58): Russian lay theologian; worked in Paris; author of *The Mystical Theology of the Eastern Church* (London, 1957; St Vladimir's Seminary Press, New York, 1976), *The Vision of God* (London, 1963), *In the Image and Likeness of God* (London/Oxford, 1975).

Macarius of Egypt, St (*c.*300–*c.*390): monk at Sketis. The *Homilies* in Greek, traditionally ascribed to him, are now considered not to be his work, and were probably written in Syria in the late 4th or early 5th century. Eng. tr. by A.J. Mason: *Fifty Spiritual Homilies of St. Macarius the Egyptian* (London, 1921).

Makarii of Optino (1788–1860): Russian *starets*. Extracts from his writings in I. de Beausobre (ed.); *Russian Letters of Direction* (London, 1944; St Vladimir's Seminary Press, New York, 1975). See also S. Bolshakoff, *Russian Mystics* (Kalamazoo/London, 1977).

Maria of Normanby, Mother (1912–77) (in the world, Lydia Gysi): Orthodox nun, German-Swiss by background;

founder of the Monastery of the Assumption, Normanby, Yorkshire; author of *The Hidden Treasure: An Orthodox Search* and *The Jesus Prayer* (both Normanby, 1972), *etc.*

Maria of Paris, Mother (1891–1945) (in the world, Elisaveta Skobtsova): Russian, at first married, then a nun; devoted her later life to social work in France; died in the Nazi concentration camp at Ravensbruck. For her life, see S. Hackel, *One, of Great Price* (London, 1965).

Mark the Monk, St (early 5th century): Greek ascetical writer. Some of his works are in *The Philokalia*, vol. i (London, 1979).

Maximus the Confessor, St (*c.* 580–662): Greek Father. Eng. tr. of his *Centuries on Love* and *Ascetic Book* by P. Sherwood (Ancient Christian Writers, vol.xxi: Washington, 1955).

Nazarii of Valamo (1735–1809): *starets*, abbot of Valamo Monastery in Finland.

Nicolas Cabasilas (c. 1322 – c. 1396): Byzantine lay theologian, author of *The Life in Christ*, tr. C.J. de Catanzaro (St Vladimir's Seminary Press, New York, 1974), and *A Commentary on the Divine Liturgy*, tr. J.M. Hussey and P.A. McNulty (London, 1960).

Nilus of Ancyra, St (early 5th century): also called (incorrectly) 'Nilus of Sinai'; Greek ascetical writer. His *Ascetic Discourse* appears in *The Philokalia*, vol.i (London, 1979).

Origen (*c.* 185 – *c.* 254): Greek Father, working chiefly at Alexandria; wrote *On Prayer*, tr. E.G. Jay (London, 1954), *etc.*

Philaret (Drozdov), Metropolitan of Moscow (1782–1867): the most eminent Russian hierarch of the 19th century; preacher and theologian. See *Select Sermons by the late Metropolitan of Moscow, Philaret*, translated anonymously (London, 1873).

Polycarp, St (c. 69 – *c.* 155): Bishop of Smyrna, martyr; in youth knew St John the Evangelist. For *The Martyrdom of Polycarp,* see M. Staniforth (tr.), *Early Christian Writings* (Penguin Classics, Harmondsworth, 1968).

Romanos the Melodist, St (early 6th century): Syrian by birth, author of many hymns in Greek. Eng. tr. by M. Carpenter, *Kontakia of Romanos, Byzantine Melodist,* 2 vols (Columbia, 1970–3).

Rozanov, Vasilii (1856–1919): Russian religious philosopher; author of *Solitaria* (London, 1927).

Sayings of the Desert Fathers, The: stories and sayings of the early monks, chiefly those of Egypt (4th–5th century). Eng. tr. by Sister Benedicta Ward: *The Sayings of the Desert Fathers. The Alphabetical Collection* (London, 1975); *The Wisdom of the Desert Fathers. Apophthegmata Patrum (The Anonymous Series)* (Fairacres Publication 48: Oxford, 1975).

Schmemann, Archpriest Alexander (born 1921): theologian of the Russian emigration, dean of St Vladimir's Orthodox Seminary in New York; author of *For the Life of the World: Sacraments and Orthodoxy* (New York, 1973) and *Of Water and the Spirit* (New York, 1974), both published by St Vladimir's Seminary Press.

Seraphim of Sarov, St (1759–1833): Russian monk and *starets*; the most famous of modern Russian saints. For his life, see I. de Beausobre, *Flame in the Snow* (London, 1945), and V. Zander, *St Seraphim of Sarov* (London, 1975). His 'Conversation with Nicolas Motovilov' is to be found in G.P. Fedotov, *A Treasury of Russian Spirituality* (London, 1950).

Sergius of Radonezh, St (c. 1314-92): the greatest national saint of Russia; founder and abbot of Holy Trinity Monastery, Zagorsk. For his life, see N. Zernov, *St Sergius – Builder of Russia* (London, no date: ?1939), and P. Kovalevsky, *St Sergius and Russian Spirituality* (St Vladimir's Seminary Press, New York, 1976).

Sherrard, Philip (born 1922): Orthodox lay theologian, living in Greece; author of *The Greek East and the Latin West* (London, 1959), *Christianity and Eros* (London, 1976), *Church, Papacy, and Schism* (London, 1978).

Staniloae. Fr Dumitru (born 1903): Romanian theologian, editor of the eight-volume Romanian translation of *The Philokalia*. See A. M. Allchin (ed.), *The Tradition of Life. Romanian Essays in Spirituality and Theology* (Fellowship of St Alban and St Sergius, London, 1971).

Symeon the New Theologian, St (949—1022): Greek ascetical and mystical writer. Eng. tr. of his *Hymns of Divine Love* by G.A. Maloney (Dimension Books, Denville, New Jersey, no date). See also Maloney, *The Mystic of Fire and Light* (same publishers, 1975).

Synesius of Cyrene (*c.* 370 – *c.* 414): Bishop of Ptolemais, Greek Father.

Theoklitos of Dionysiou, Fr: contemporary Greek monk on Athos; author of books on monasticism and prayer.

Theophan the Recluse, Bishop (1815–94): Russian spiritual writer. Edited *Unseen Warfare*, Eng. tr. E. Kadloubovsky and G.E.H. Palmer (London, 1952); extracts from his letters in Igumen Chariton, *The Art of Prayer: An Orthodox Anthology*, Eng. tr. E. Kadloubovsky and E.M. Palmer (London, 1966).

Theophilus of Antioch (late 2nd century): Greek theologian, one of the 'Apologists'. Author of *Apology to Autolycus*, Eng. tr. by R.M. Grant (Oxford, 1970).

Tikhon of Zadonsk, St (1724–83): Bishop of Voronezh, Russian spiritual writer and preacher. See N. Gorodetzky, *Saint Tikhon Zadonsky* (London, 1951).

Varsanuphius, St (early 6th century): monk of Gaza; recluse and spiritual father. Extracts from his letters in D.J. Chitty, *The Desert a City* (London, 1966).

Vladimir Monomakh, Prince of Kiev (1053 – 1125): **Russian**

ruler.

Way of a Pilgrim, The: anonymous autobiographical work, dating from the mid 19th century; recounts the wanderings of a Russian pilgrim who practises the continual recitation of the Jesus Prayer. Translated by R.M. French (London, 1954).

Zachariah, Fr (1850–1936): *starets* at the Trinity–St Sergius Monastery, Zagorsk, Russia. For his life, see *An Early Soviet Saint,* tr. Jane Ellis (London/Oxford, 1976).

(II)

NON-ORTHODOX

Boehme, Jacob (1575–1624): German Lutheran mystical writer, author of *The Way to Christ,* tr. Peter Erb (The Classics of Western Spirituality, N.Y., 1978), *etc.*

Book of the Poor in Spirit, The: German mystical treatise of the 14th century; Eng. tr. by C.F. Kelley (London, 1954):

Cloud of Unknowing, The: English mystical treatise of the 14th century, deeply influenced by St Dionysius the Areopagite. See W. Johnston, *The Mysticism of the Cloud of Unknowing. A Modern Interpretation* (N.Y., 1967).

Eckhart, Meister (c. 1260 – 1327): German Dominican mystical writer. Eng. tr. of selected writings by R.B. Blakney (Harper Torchbooks, N.Y., 1941).

Julian of Norwich, The Lady (c. 1342 – after 1413): English mystical writer, author of the *Showings* or *Revelations of Divine Love:* new ed. by E. Colledge and J. Walsh (The

Classics of Western Spirituality, N.Y., 1978).

Law, William (1686–1761): Anglican Nonjuror and spiritual writer. See *Selected Mystical Writings of William Law,* ed. S. Hobhouse (London, 1938).

Lewis, C.S. (1898–1963): Anglican, author of *The Problem of Pain* (London, 1940), *etc.*

Merton, Thomas (1915–68): Roman Catholic Cistercian writer in the USA, author of *The Sign of Jonas* (London, 1953), *Conjectures of a Guilty Bystander* (Image Books, New York, 1968), *etc.*

New Clairvaux, Monk of: author of *Don't You Belong to Me?* (Paulist Press, N.Y., 1979).

Newman, John Henry Cardinal (1801–90): leader of the Anglican Tractarians; became a Roman Catholic in 1845; author of *The Arians of the Fourth Century* (1833) and other works on the Fathers.

Suso, Henry (c. 1295–1366): German Dominican mystical writer. See *The Life of Blessed Henry Suso by Himself,* tr. T.F. Knox (London, 1913).

Thompson, Francis (1859–1907): Roman Catholic poet.

Traherne, Thomas (c. 1636–74): English mystical poet and spiritual writer; author of *Centuries of Meditations.*

Tyrrell, George (1861–1909): Roman Catholic writer linked with the Modernist movement.

INDEX

AUTHORS AND SOURCES

Abraham Yaakov of Sadagora, 70

Agathon, Abba, 140, 151

Andrew of Crete, St, 180, 186

Antony of Egypt, St, 12, 54, 142, 143, 146, 186

Antony, Metropolitan of Kiev, 105, 186

Aphrahat, 42, 52, 186

Arsenius, Abba, 172

Athanasius of Alexandria, St, 27, 186

Augustine, St, 22, 59, 108, 186

Basil the Great, St, 27, 43, 71, 93, 186
  Liturgy of, 103, 109

Beausobre, Iulia de, 86, 131, 186

Berdyaev, Nicolas, 73, 186

Betjeman, John, 9

Blake, William, 14–15, 158

Boehme, Jacob, 172, 194

Book of the Poor in Spirit, 83, 194

Brianchaninov: *see* Ignatii

Bulgakov, Sergius, 79, 187

Cabasilas: *see* Nicolas Cabasilas

Christmas, hymns for, 94, 98, 103, 114

Chrysostom: *see* John Chrysostom

Clement of Alexandria, St, 71, 169, 187

Clément, Olivier, 22, 86, 159, 187

Climacus: *see* John Climacus

Cloud of Unknowing, 20, 194

Colliander, Tito, 48, 151, 172, 173, 187

Cyril of Alexandria, St, 103, 187

Cyril of Jerusalem, St, 182, 187

Desert Fathers: see Sayings of the Desert Fathers

Diadochus of Photike, St, 175, 187

Dimitrii of Rostov, St, 21, 187

Dionysius the Areopagite, St, 31, 141, 169, 172, 187

Dostoevsky, Feodor, 73, 81, 108, 127, 128, 187

Duns Scotus, 92

Eckhart, Meister, 153, 194

Elchaninov, Alexander, 144, 187

Eliot, T.S., 88

Ephrem the Syrian, St, 103, 115, 162, 188

Ephiphany, Blessing of the Waters at, 84

Eriugena, John Scotús, 29, 188

Evagrius of Pontus, 12, 54, 59, 141, 156, 163, 170, 173, 188

Evdokimov, Paul, 76, 86, 153, 188

Festal Menaion, 53, 188

Florovsky, George, 7, 188

Friday, hymns for Great, 116

Gospel of Truth, 152

Gregory of Nyssa, St, 16, 30, 38–39, 59, 141, 164, 169, 176, 185, 188

Gregory Palamas, St, 58, 170, 177, 188

Gregory the Theologian, St, 40, 99, 170, 188

Hasidim, 63, 70
Herbert, George, 160
Hermas, 118, 189
Hopkins, Gerard Manley, 120

Ignatii (Brianchaninov), 147, 189
Ioannikios, St, 33, 189
Irenaeus of Lyons, St, 44, 64, 66, 183, 185, 189
Isaac the Syrian, St, 51, 61, 71, 72, 88, 92–93, 134, 146, 152, 156–7, 174, 178, 182, 189
Isaias of Sketis, St, 152, 184, 189

James, Liturgy of St, 39
John Chrysostom, St, 50, 111, 189
    Liturgy of, 46, 55, 69
John Climacus, St, 87, 166, 189
John of Damascus, St, 43, 189
John of Kronstadt, St, 51, 55, 114, 189
Joseph of Panepho, Abba, 35–36
Julian of Norwich, 42, 59, 110, 194

Kallistos Kataphygiotis, 32, 190
Khomiakov, Aleksei, 81, 143, 190

Law, William, 105, 195
Lenten Triodion, 33, 50, 51, 83, 190
Leo the Great, St, 96
Leontius of Cyprus, St, 70, 190
Lewis, C.S., 60, 153, 195
Lossky, Vladimir, 34, 85, 138, 171, 190

Macarius of Egypt, St, 25, 68, 149, 168, 170, 171, 177, 178, 182, 190
Makarii of Optino, 175, 190
Maria of Normanby, Mother, 113, 115, 175, 190

Maria of Paris, Mother, 51, 52, 113, 191
Mark the Monk, St, 87, 138, 149, 173, 191
Maugham, Somerset, 73
Maximus the Confessor, St, 31, 59, 92, 98, 141, 171, 191
Merton, Thomas, 19, 71, 195

Nazarii of Valamo, 150, 191
New Clairvaux, Monk of, 58, 195
Newman, J.H., 17, 185, 195
Nicolas Cabasilas, 13, 14, 25, 144, 146, 191
Nilus of Ancyra, St, 86, 191

Origen, 54, 66, 114, 141, 170, 191

Pambo, Abba, 172
Pascal, Blaise, 22
Pentecost, hymns for, 51, 122, 125, 137, 139
Philaret, Metropolitan of Moscow, 8, 57, 147, 191
Philo, 169
Polycarp, St, 20–21, 192

Raine, Kathleen, 33, 63
Robinson, J.A.T., 19
Romanos the Melodist, St, 94, 192
Rozanov, Vasilii, 140, 192
Ruskin, John, 153

Sarapion the Sindonite, St, 7
Sayings of the Desert Fathers, 12, 35, 48, 68, 88, 112, 140, 142, 143, 146, 150, 151, 154, 171, 178, 192
Schmemann, Alexander, 112, 192
Seraphim of Sarov, St, 118, 129–31, 151, 192
Sergius of Radonezh, St, 49, 192
Shakespeare, William, 33
Shaw, George Bernard, 54

Sherrard, Philip, 67, 193
Sisois, Abba, 143
Staniloae, Dumitru, 69, 85, 87, 116, 193
Suso, Henry, 160, 195
Symeon the New Theologian, St, 12, 21, 30, 32, 68, 119, 137, 170, 193
Synesius of Cyrene, 41, 193

Talmud, 62, 64
Theoklitos, Fr, 52, 174, 193
Theophan the Recluse, 151, 172, 193
Theophilus of Antioch, 31, 193
Thompson, Francis, 29, 195

Tikhon of Zadonsk, St, 148, 193
Tolkien, J.R.R., 184
Tolstoy, Leo, 10
Traherne, Thomas, 24, 195
Tyrrell, George, 13, 195

Varsanuphius, St, 72, 193
Vaughan, Henry, 172
Vladimir Monomakh, 24, 193

Way of a Pilgrim, 166, 194
Wesley, John, 22
Williams, Charles, 35

Zachariah, Fr, 127–31, 194
Zosima, *Starets*, 81, 108

SUBJECTS

Abraham, 15
Active life, 142
Age to come, 178–85
Angels, 62–63, 74
Animals:
  compared with man, 60–61
  in Age to come, 183
Antichrist, 179–80
Apatheia, 156
Apollinarianism, 99
Apophatic approach, 16–17,
  162–3, 167
Arians, 96
Asceticism, 79–80, 156
Assumption of Virgin Mary,
  103
Augustinian view of fall, 81,
  102

Baptism:
  of Christ, 45, 123
  of Christian, 132–3, 137–8,
  145
Bible, 130, 146–9, 162
Body, the human, 60, 64, 79,
  155–6, 176
  see Resurrection

Calvinism, 80
Cataphatic approach, 163
  see Apophatic approach
Chrismation, 133
Christ: *see* Jesus Christ
Church:
  as ikon of Trinity, 49
  and love, 51
  and Holy Spirit, 138
  membership of, 143–4
Communion, Holy: *see*
  Eucharist
Confession, 128
Confirmation, 133
Contemplation, 141, 157–62
  contemplative and active
  life, 142

Councils, the seven
  Ecumenical, 36, 94–95
Creation, 44, 55–58
  ex nihilo, 55
  continual, 57
Cross, 83, 88, 104–10, 151, 173–
  4

Darkness, the divine, 15–17,
  31, 141, 169–70, 175–6
Death, 64, 77–78, 104, 113, 143
Deification of man, 28, 98, 146,
  167
Demons, 57, 74–75, 135
Diakrisis, 154
Discernment of spirits, 135
Discrimination, 154
Dispassion, 156, 174
Doubt, 19
Dualism, 58–59

Elder: *see* Spiritual father
Energies, the divine, 27–28, 31,
  158, 167–9
Epektasis, 185
Epiclesis, 46, 118, 124
Epiphany, 45, 84, 123
Essence of God, 37, 95–96,
  167–8
  see Energies
Eternal life, 183–5
Eucharist, 46, 48, 69, 85, 145–6
Evil, 23, 59–60, 73–76, 86
Evolution, 67
Experience, personal, 8, 22,
  134–5

Faith, 18–19, 27
Fall, 74–81
  and Incarnation, 92–93, 99–
  100
  and Virgin Mary, 102
Fasting, 156
Father, God the, 39–40
Filioque, 40, 122
  see Spirit

Flesh, 79
Fools in Christ, 131–2
Free will, 61, 65, 75–76, 105, 149, 181

Geron, 127
Gethsemane, 105
Gnostics, 59
God:
  nearness yet otherness, 13–14
  as mystery, 14–18, 29–31
  as personal, 18–20
  experience of, 22
  existence of, three pointers, 22–26
  unity in diversity, 36–39
  God and suffering, 82–83, 95
  see Darkness, Energies, Essence, Light, Love, Trinity
Grace and free will, 149

Healing, spiritual, 127
Heart, 25, 154–5, 165
Hell, 35, 57, 106, 181–2
Hesychia, 163
Holy Spirit: *see* Spirit
Homoousios, 36, 94
Hypostasis, 37, 168
  see Person

Ikons, 9, 69, 95, 161
Image, human beings in God's, 49, 64–68, 69, 81, 84, 93
  distinguished from likeness, 66
Immaculate Conception, 102
Incarnation, 44, 82, 92–99, 104, 110, 123, 168
Intellect, spiritual, 61, 154, 165
Iurodivyi, 131

Jesus Christ, 88–117
  true God, 36, 89–90, 94, 96–97
  true man, 89–90, 94–97
  two natures and wills, 94–95

  human soul of, 99
  takes fallen human nature, 99–100
  as Saviour, 90
  as Christ or Messiah, 91
  see Baptism, Cross, Incarnation, Resurrection, Transfiguration
Jesus Prayer, 48, 90–91, 112, 164–6, 175
Joy, 112, 118
Judgement, the Last, 52, 181

Kenosis, 109
Kingdom, the inner, 70–72, 86

Last Day, 64, 78, 178–83
Light, the divine, 15, 21, 30, 169–72, 177
Likeness, the divine: *see* Image
Logos, logoi, 40–41, 61, 158
Love:
  within God, 33–35
  of God for creation, 56, 75, 85, 181–2
  of man for God, 20, 32, 51
  between human persons, 25–26, 34–35, 48–49, 52, 81–82, 86
  as 'ecstatic', 32, 56, 92
  and freedom, 75–76
  and suffering, 83
  and lust, 156
  victory of, 107–10

Man: *see* Person, the human
Manichaeans, 58
Marriage, 79
Mary, the Blessed Virgin, 44–45, 88, 94, 100–3, 118, 120, 123
Metanoia, 17, 34, 131, 152
  see Repentance
Microcosm, man as, 54, 62–64, 86, 183
Monasticism, 79
Moses, 15, 17, 141, 158, 171, 175

Mother, Holy Spirit as, 42
Myron, 133
Mystery, meaning of word, 17–18
   God as mystery, 14–18, 27, 30–31

Names, given by Adam, 69
Nature, contemplation of, 141, 157–62
   and Scripture, 162
Negative theology: *see* Apophatic approach
Nepsis, 152, 157
Nous, 61

Orans, 118
Original sin, 77–81, 102
Ousia, 37
   see Essence

Pain, 73, 77
Panentheism, 58, 158
Passions, 155
Pentecost, 123–6
Pentecostal movement, 134–6
Perichoresis, 34
Person:
   God as personal, 13, 19–20, 33–35, 37–38
   person, the human, 60–72
   and mutual love, 34, 67–68
   tripartite division of man, 60–61
   man as microcosm, 54, 62–64, 86, 183
   man as mediator, 63–64, 183
Physiki, 141
Platonism, 59
Praktiki, 141
Prayer, 140–77
   nothing so difficult, 140, 151
   daily prayers, 46–48
   three stages, 140–3
   prayer of the heart, 154–5, 165
   pure prayer, 86
   self-acting prayer, 165

prayer and contemplation, 157–62
   and silence, 163
   and humility, 174
   and thanksgiving, 55
   and social service, 52
   see Jesus Prayer
Priest of creation, man as, 68–70, 85
Prosopon, 37
   see Person

Repentance, 143, 151–2
   see Metanoia
Resurrection:
   of Christ, 110–12, 116–17, 151, 182
   of body, 64, 78, 87, 146, 180–3

Sacraments, 144–6
   see Baptism, Chrismation, Confession, Eucharist
Sacrifice, 85
   of Christ, 104, 110
Salos, 131
Salvation, two principles of, 96
   as sharing, 97–98, 104–5
Scripture: *see* Bible
Second Coming of Christ, 179–80
Silence, 163, 178
Sin, 72, 75, 77, 90–1
   see Evil
Sobriety, 136
Son, God the, 40–42, 44–46
   see Jesus Christ
Soul, 60–61
   Christ has a human soul, 99
Spirit, the Holy, 9, 61, 118–39
   as a person, 121
   as true God, 36, 122
   as mother, 42
   procession of, 40–41, 43, 121–2
   at creation, 44
   and the human spirit, 61
   and Christ, 44–46, 123–4

204

at Pentecost, 123–6
in the Eucharist, 46, 124
conscious awareness of, 134
and divine Light, 176–7
Spirit, the human, 60–61
Spiritual father, 127–31, 135,
146
Starets, 127
Suffering, 73–75, 82–83, 87
of God, 82–83, 95, 105
of Christ, 95, 104–5
Symbols, 16, 42–43

Tears, 87, 134–5
Temptation, 143, 154, 156
Theanthropos, 91
Theologia, 141
Theosis: see Deification
Theotokos, 94, 101
Tongues, speaking with, 134–5
Tradition, Holy, 9, 148

Transfiguration:
of Christ, 45, 106, 110, 123,
151, 170, 182
of human person, 171–2
of material creation, 183
Trinity, 33–53, 67–68, 75, 81,
95–96, 97, 167–8

Union with God, 166–9

Virgin Birth, 100–3
see Mary
Vision of God, 141, 170–2, 176–
7

Watchfulness, 152, 157
Way, Christianity as the, 7–8
Will:
Trinity has one, 37, 96
Christ has two, 95